"A faithful source of biblical clear-headedness and a model for preaching that shapes our palette for the deep things of God and his gospel."

John Starke, Lead Pastor, All Souls Church, New York, New York;
editor, The Gospel Coalition

SETTING
OUR AFFECTIONS
UPON GLORY

SETTING OUR AFFECTIONS UPON GLORY

NINE SERMONS ON THE GOSPEL AND THE CHURCH

MARTYN LLOYD-JONES

:: CROSSWAY®

WHEATON, ILLINOIS

Setting Our Affections upon Glory

Copyright © 2013 by Elizabeth Catherwood and Ann Beatt

Published by Crossway
      1300 Crescent Street
      Wheaton, Illinois 60187

Cover design: Studio Gearbox

Cover image: Getty Images

First printing 2013

Printed in the United States of America

Scripture quotations are from the *King James Version* of the Bible.

All emphases in Scripture quotations have been added by the author.

Trade paperback ISBN: 978-1-4335-3265-8
PDF ISBN: 978-1-4335-3266-5
Mobipocket ISBN: 978-1-4335-3275-7
ePub ISBN: 978-1-4335-3287-0

Library of Congress Cataloging-in-Publication Data

Lloyd-Jones, David Martyn.
   Setting our affections upon glory : nine sermons on the
      Gospel and the church / Martyn Lloyd-Jones.
      p. cm.
   Includes bibliographical references.
   ISBN 978-1-4335-3265-8 (tp)
     1. Bible. N.T.—Sermons. 2. Sermons, English—20th
century. I. Title.
BS2341.55.L56   2013
252'.058—dc23   2012003831

Crossway is a publishing ministry of Good News Publishers.

CH   27 26 25 24 23 22 21 20 19 18 17

CONTENTS

FOREWORD

✹

I heard the sermons included in this volume in 1969 while a university student. During Christmas break the young adult minister at my home church encouraged me to attend the Pensacola Theological Institute. At the time I doubted I would be able to go because this institute was usually scheduled for late August, which conflicted with the start of the academic year. This year, however, the institute was earlier than usual.

A young lady from church and I took the bus from Miami to Pensacola and arrived Sunday morning. As we went through the bus station to catch a cab to McIlwain Memorial Presbyterian Church, host of the Pensacola Theological Institute, I looked at the morning paper. A map of the Gulf Coast showed an area under a hurricane warning. In the middle of that area was Pensacola.

The service planned for that Sunday evening, August 17, was moved up to 2:00 P.M. so everyone could be in homes by the time Hurricane Camille struck the city. This was the service when Dr. Martyn Lloyd-Jones preached the sermon "The Acid Test." By that time the hurricane had begun to turn west, sparing Pensacola, reaching landfall in Mississippi instead. I had the impression for years that the sermon was not in the Doctor's plan but was one he had used during the Blitz and thought appropriate for the occasion.

The Sunday services, as well as the weekday morning lectures by other faculty members, were held at McIlwain. Due to the expected crowds eager to hear Dr. Lloyd-Jones, the weekday evening services were held in the much larger facilities of a Baptist church in downtown Pensacola. On Friday afternoon they had a fish fry on the beach, during which I had the opportunity to thank Dr. Lloyd-Jones for his messages.

Though the Pensacola Theological Institute was open to Christians in general, it seemed that a significant portion of the attendees were ministers. A number of ministers and laymen, who a few years later would form the Presbyterian Church in America, attended this conference each year.

The church had arranged for all messages to be recorded and then made available for purchase. I bought the full set in 1969. Some years ago, when my reel-to-reel tape deck was still functional, I made it a point to digitize Dr. Lloyd-Jones's sermons. Recently I made these recordings available to the Martyn Lloyd-Jones Recordings Trust, and now these sermons are being put in print for the first time.

John Schultz
Germantown, Tennessee

1

THE ACID TEST[1]

✳

> For our light affliction, which is but for a moment, worketh for us a far more exceeding and eternal weight of glory; while we look not at the things which are seen, but at the things which are not seen: for the things which are seen are temporal; but the things which are not seen are eternal.
>
> 2 CORINTHIANS 4:17–18

In the last two verses of the fourth chapter of the second epistle of Paul to the Corinthians, the apostle Paul brings to a kind of grand climax the series of amazing and astonishing things that he has just been saying. This is, undoubtedly, one of the great statements in the Scriptures, one of those nuggets that we find standing out here and there, especially in the writings of the great apostle Paul. There are variations even in the writings of the holy men of God who were guided and controlled as they wrote the Scriptures, and this is undoubtedly one of the most eloquent and moving passages.

I say that in order that I may issue a warning. I always feel, when we read a passage like 2 Corinthians 4, that there is a very real danger that we should be so affected and moved and carried away by the eloquence, the diction, the style, the balance that we pay no attention to the message. This is true, I think, of many psalms. There are people who read the psalms not to get their message but because of the beauty of the language and the diction. Some people, it seems, even use them as a kind of soporific. Carried away by the lilt and the cadence and the beauty of the language, they pay no attention at all to the meaning. So I feel, always, when we handle such a passage that we have to take ourselves in hand, discipline ourselves, and make certain that we do lay hold of the message.

We must remember that this great apostle was not a literary man. We must not think of him as a man in a study surrounded by his books, sitting down to produce a great masterpiece of literature or eloquence. That is not the case at all. This man was a preacher, an evangelist, a pastor, a teacher, a founder of churches. So when he produces a great passage like this, it is something almost accidental. What happened was that he was so moved and so carried away that he found himself writing like this almost unconsciously. We must bear that in mind lest we miss the message and be affected by the sound of the language and the beauty of the passage merely from the standpoint of literature.

I emphasize this because actually the apostle here was writing in very difficult conditions. Literary men, such as the poets, generally need to have favorable circumstances before they can produce their best work. I remember a postcard that G. K. Chesterton sent to a friend of mine who had written to him asking, "Why is it that the poets can be so glorious in their poetry but often are so disappointing in their personal lives and in their beliefs and in their prose?" Chesterton's reply was this: "Poets often sing what they cannot say." And that, it seems to me, is the exact antithesis of what is true of the man of God, the true Christian. If we cannot say these things as well as sing them, there is very little value in them. So here is the apostle Paul, a man writing out of the midst of great troubles—he even gives us a list of them—and yet surrounded as he is by trials and tribulations, this is what he is able to say: "For our light affliction, which is but for a moment, worketh for us a far more exceeding and eternal weight of glory."

Now I want to consider these two verses with you because I believe that a great need in the Christian church today is for a body of people who can speak as Paul does. I think this is also the supreme need of our world as it is at the present time, full of so much uncertainty and toil and trouble. I believe the church and the world are waiting for a body of people who can take their stand by the side of this apostle and join him in making this great declaration. So it would be good for us to examine ourselves in the light of this statement. Is this our attitude toward our modern world? Is this how we are facing the present and the unknown future, which is so full of foreboding?

Let me put it to you like this. I am suggesting that in these two verses we have the acid test of our profession of the Christian faith. When I say *acid test*, I mean the most delicate, the most sensitive test, the test of tests. Let us imagine that I put the following question to you: What is the acid test of any man or woman's profession of the Christian faith?

I can imagine someone without any hesitation saying, "That's perfectly simple. No problem there. My acid test is the test of orthodoxy. It's obvious. If a man does not believe certain things, he is clearly not a Christian. He may be a good man, but if he does not believe a certain irreducible minimum, he cannot, in fact, call himself a Christian. Whatever else he may be, a man who doesn't believe in God, in the being of God, is not a Christian. If he doesn't believe in the deity of the Lord Jesus Christ, his incarnation, his miracles, his atoning death, his physical resurrection, his ascension, the sending of the Holy Spirit and the person of the Spirit, why, if he doesn't believe these things, he just cannot be a Christian. The test is orthodoxy."

What do we say to that? I think we must agree at once that the test of orthodoxy is not only a valuable test, it is vitally important. I agree a hundred percent. Unless a man does believe this irreducible minimum, he just cannot be a Christian. And yet while I say that, I am not prepared to accept the test of orthodoxy as the acid test of one's Christian profession for this reason: as we know from history, perhaps some of us from personal experience, it is quite possible to be perfectly orthodox and yet to be spiritually dead. There is such a thing, after all, as having or giving an intellectual assent to the truth. There have been people in the church who have been thoroughly orthodox—they have accepted biblical teaching, they have believed it all, they have often fought for it—and yet it can be said of them, in the words of Paul, that while "having a form of godliness," they are "denying the power thereof" (2 Tim. 3:5). Many have denied in their daily lives what they have professed and claimed to believe on Sundays. They have been quite orthodox, but at the same time without life, without power. Because of the terrible danger of a mere intellectual assent, orthodoxy, while it is absolutely essential, is not sufficiently delicate to merit the designation of *acid test*.

Then I see someone hurriedly saying, "You're perfectly right. To me the acid test of whether or not people are Christians is not so much what they say as the life they live. That's the test. Speech is easy. The question is, are they moral? Are they upright? Are they philanthropic? Behavior and morality—this, to me, proclaims what people are."

What do we say here? Of course, we agree at once that conduct is an absolutely vital test. If people do not live this life, then no matter what they may profess, clearly they are not Christians. The Scriptures make this terribly plain and clear to us in so many passages. The life lived is absolutely vital. Morality is an essential part of this Christian faith of ours. And yet, though I say that, I again must hurry to say that I will not accept this either as our acid test. This point is particularly important at the present time, when the popular and prevailing view is that conduct is the acid test. But we cannot agree to that for this good reason: there are many men and women who live highly moral and ethical lives in this world, people who do much good and are great benefactors of the human race, yet who cannot be called Christians. Why not? Because they deny God himself and the very elements of this faith. There are many humanists and others against whom you cannot bring any criticism on moral grounds; you cannot point a finger at them. So if you judge merely by behavior, if you put this up as the acid test and say that belief is unnecessary, you are denying the whole of the Christian faith. Morality is essential, but it is not enough. It does not constitute the acid test.

Then I imagine a third person coming forward and saying, "Well, I'm still in agreement with you, and I wouldn't have suggested either of those tests. No, it's quite simple. The acid test is the test of experience. That's the vital thing. What I want to know about people who make a profession is this: Can they say, 'Whereas I once was blind, now I see'? Has there been some great crisis, some climactic experience in their lives that has turned them around and made new people of them? This is the vital thing, the test of experience."

Here, again, is a most important test. No one is born a Christian. You have to be born again to become a Christian. Experience is a vital part of our whole position. I am not postulating that you must have some standard experience, that you must be able to point to a particular moment and a particular preacher, a particular text, and so on. But I am postulating that men and women who are Christians are aware that the Spirit of God has been dealing with them and has done something vital to them. They are aware that they have new life within them. Experience is essential. Yet I am not prepared to accept this either as what I am calling the acid test of our profession, for this obvious reason—and again it is so important at this present time: if you make the test of experience the acid test, what have you to say to the many cults that are flourishing round and about us? After all these cults give people experiences. I am thinking of cults such as Christian Science. One of the most dramatic changes I have ever seen in a person's life was in the case of a lady who became a Christian Scientist. She was entirely changed and transformed—a great experience! Obviously the cults emphasize experiences. They would not succeed if it were not for this. They obviously have something to give to people, otherwise they would not be flourishing. So if we put up experience as the ultimate standard, the acid test, we are left without any reply at all to these various cults. Experience is essential, but it is not enough. It is not delicate and sensitive enough to merit the term *acid test*.

"Well," says somebody, "if you're rejecting all these tests, what's your test?"

Let me suggest it to you. My test is the test we have in these two verses that we are considering. Why is this the acid test? It is because it includes the other three tests, covers them, and guarantees them. In other words, I am suggesting that the acid test of our profession is our total response to life, to everything that takes place within us and around us. Not partial but total. And this, I emphasize, is a guarantee of these other aspects to which I have been referring.

During the last war,[2] in my ministry in London I often used to say that what determines whether or not you and I are Christians is not what we say on vacation and not what we say when we are in our studies or reading a book somewhere and reading about theology and reading the Scriptures. That is not the ultimate test. The acid test of our profession is this: What do you feel like when you are sitting in an air-raid shelter and you can hear the bombs dropping round and about you, and you know that the next bomb may land on you and may be the end of you? That is the test. How do you feel when you are face-to-face with the ultimate, with the end? Or I might put it in terms of young men engaged in action on the field of battle. What is your response as you are facing life and death and all the great ultimate questions? What is your reaction? Or, coming nearer home, let me put it like this: the ultimate test of our profession of the Christian faith is what we feel, what we say, and what our reaction is when a hurricane comes[3] or a tornado or some calamity produced by nature or some violent epidemic, a disease that brings us face-to-face with time and eternity, with life and death. The ultimate question is, what is our response then? Because that is exactly what the apostle is saying here.

Paul is surrounded by many troubles and trials and problems. They could not have been worse. Yet he looks at them all and says, "For our light affliction, which is but for a moment, worketh for us a far more exceeding and eternal weight of glory." Do we react like that as we look at the worst, as we look at life at its darkest and its starkest? I suggest that this is the acid test because, you see, it covers my orthodoxy. The only people who can speak like this are those who know whom they have believed, those who are certain of their faith. Nobody else can. Other people can turn their backs upon disasters and whistle to keep up their courage in the dark, they can do many things, but they cannot speak like this without being orthodox. This test also guarantees conduct and morality, because the trouble with people who merely have an intellectual belief is that in the moment of crisis their faith does not help them. They feel condemned. Their consciences accuse them. They are in trouble because they know they are frauds. And in the same way this test also guarantees the experiential element, the life, the power, the vigor. People cannot speak like this unless these truths are living realities to them. They are the only ones who are able to look upon calamity and smile at it and refer to it as "our light affliction, which is but for a moment," which "worketh for us a far more exceeding and eternal weight of glory."

So here is the great test for us. Can we speak like this? Do we speak like this? We may be orthodox. That is not enough. We may be good people. That is not enough. We may have had some great thrilling experience. That is not enough. How do we stand up to the ultimate questions? We have seen the apostle's answer, and the question I now want to put to you briefly is this: What was it that made him write in this way and manner? What is the explanation of his ability to face all these things? He has given us a list of his trials. "We are troubled," he says, "on every side . . . we are perplexed . . . persecuted . . . cast down . . . always bearing about in the body the dying of the Lord Jesus . . . . We which live are always delivered unto death for Jesus' sake" (2 Cor. 4:8–11). And yet, having given us the list, this is what the apostle says: "our light affliction, which is but for a moment." What enabled him to say this?

Now, once more, many people at the present time would come to us and say there is no problem there at all. They say, "Surely this is just a matter of temperament." Someone will say, "I'm a psychologist, and I discovered in my reading of psychology that there are different types of temperament, different types of personality. Some people are born optimists, some are pessimists. Some have a depressive, pessimistic outlook; others are sanguine by temperament. There are people who always see a silver lining in every cloud. It does not matter how dark things may look, such people always smile, and they say, 'It's all right. Don't be depressed. Things will get better. This isn't the end, you know.' They are born optimists. They are like corks. It does not matter what happens, they keep on bobbing up to the surface. And no doubt," says this person, "your apostle Paul was a man who happened to be born with this sanguine, optimistic temperament. That's why he refused to be discouraged and depressed and kept on being cheerful in spite of everything."

But anybody who knows anything about the apostle Paul knows

that this is entirely wrong as an explanation of his language for, beyond any question, by nature and temperament the apostle Paul was a depressive person, a man who could be easily discouraged. These Corinthians had depressed him and discouraged him. They had made insulting remarks about him. They had said, "His bodily presence is weak, and his speech contemptible" (2 Cor. 10:10). They had hurt him grievously, and he tells us in chapter 7 of this very epistle, "When we were come into Macedonia, our flesh had no rest, but we were troubled on every side; without were fightings, within were fears" (v. 5). Paul was about as far removed as is possible from your natural optimist, the person with a sanguine temperament. No, no! This is not psychology. And thank God it is not. If the gospel of Jesus Christ were merely something that enables the natural optimist to speak as Paul does at the end of 2 Corinthians 4, then what would happen to those of us who are natural pessimists? No, the glory of the gospel is this—it can come to men and women of every conceivable type of temperament and outlook and enable them to speak like this. It does not depend upon us as we are by nature. It depends upon what the gospel has done to us. Psychology is not the explanation.

"All right," says somebody, "if it isn't temperament, surely it must be that the apostle Paul had espoused a particular philosophical outlook."

The apostle lived in an age when there was a popular philosophy that went under the name of Stoicism. We read in the seventeenth chapter of Acts that when the apostle went to Athens, he found there people called Stoics and Epicureans. These were the two main schools of ancient philosophy. Stoicism was the philosophy of courage, the philosophy of grit, the philosophy of "sticking to it." The Stoic was a very wise and thoughtful man, unlike the Epicurean, whose philosophy, in a general sense, was, "Let us eat, drink, and be merry, for tomorrow we die," the philosophy of pleasure. The Stoic said, "No, no! You must think. You must face the facts of life." And he had done so. He was a really able and intelligent kind of person. The Stoic had meditated seriously about life and its problems, and he had come to the conclusion that if you want to go through life successfully, if you want to end standing on your feet, if you want to get through undefeated, there is only one way to do it: you must brace your shoulders; you must have a firm upper lip; you must clench your teeth; you must take yourself in hand; you must exercise discipline and have an iron will; you must refuse to be defeated. If you do not, you will go down. And many have thought that the explanation of the apostle's language here is that he had become a Stoic.

Now this, to me, is most important because, unless I am very greatly mistaken, large numbers of people in the Christian church today are confusing Stoicism with Christianity. We certainly saw a great deal of Stoicism in England, and in London, during World War II. For that reason I was constantly preaching on this theme. We had a slogan: "London can take it." *Let the Germans come and bomb us, London can take it.* But I want to show you that Stoicism is the exact opposite of Christianity, that it has nothing to do with it. Why is that? Because there is this great difference: the philosophy of Stoicism is the philosophy of resignation. It is the philosophy of putting up with it, taking it, simply standing and refusing to give in. Stoicism is negative, whereas the very essence of Christianity is that it is positive. Christians are not people who are just bearing with things and putting up with them. They are triumphing. They are exulting. They are "more than conquerors" (Rom. 8:37).

Let me make this point plain and clear by quoting to you two pieces of poetry, one of them an expression of the philosophy of Stoicism, the other an expression of the true Christian position. Look at Stoicism first. Here are a few lines from the English poet John Dryden, who I think has given the perfect expression to the philosophy of Stoicism. This is how he puts it:

> Since every man who lives is born to die,
> And none can boast sincere felicity,
> With equal mind, what happens, let us bear,
> Nor joy nor grieve too much for things beyond our care.
> Like pilgrims to th' appointed place we tend;
> The world's an inn, and death the journey's end.

That is perfect Stoicism. "Every man who lives is born to die." That is a profound observation, and the trouble with most people in the world today is that they never realize that. That is why they get so terrified when they hear warnings about hurricanes and tornadoes. They never think of death. They assume they are going to live in this world forever. But the Stoic has thought. He has faced the facts. "Every man who lives is born to die."

And then Dryden goes on to say, "And none can boast sincere felicity," by which he means that there is no such thing in this world as sincere, unmixed felicity or happiness. There is nobody who is perfectly happy. There is always a fly in the ointment, always something lacking. So what do you do about it? And here is the answer: "With equal mind." It is the philosophy of balance, the philosophy of discipline, of control, the philosophy of maintaining an even keel: "what happens, let us bear, nor joy nor grieve too much for things beyond our care." If you want to be happy in this world and to go through it triumphantly, says the Stoic, you must control your feelings. Never be too happy because you never know what is coming around the corner. But, on the other hand, he says, never be too unhappy: "Nor joy nor grieve too much for things beyond our care." Keep yourself under control. This was the philosophy of Thomas Arnold, the headmaster of Rugby School in England, who popularized the nineteenth-century school ethos of "the little gentleman" who curbs his feelings, holds them in, never shows them.

"Nor joy nor grieve too much for things beyond our care." Why? Well, says Dryden, it comes to this: "Like pilgrims to th' appointed place we tend." What is life? It is a pilgrimage. We are a body of pilgrims, and we are moving on; you cannot go back. And there is the pressure of the crowd behind us. We are being pushed on day by day. What is the world? Dryden says it is a sort of "inn," a kind of hotel in which you stay overnight and pay your bill in the morning and go on. "The world's an inn, and death the journey's end." That is it. A life of trouble, of toils and problems and difficulties, things battering you and beating upon you. If you exercise great courage and iron will, you will get through it, but at the end there is only death. That is the end, and there is no more. But stand up to it. Do not give in. Do not whimper and cry. Hold yourself in check. That was Stoicism.

I am trying to show you that what the apostle says here is not

Stoicism. It is, as I have said, the exact opposite. So I quote now from a second piece of poetry, written by a man named H. G. Spafford, who lived in the city of Chicago in the nineteenth century. Spafford was a successful and wealthy attorney. Moreover, he was a fine Christian man with a wife and four daughters. One year it was decided that Mrs. Spafford and the girls should pay a visit to Europe, to be joined later by Mr. Spafford, who was not able to leave with them. He took them, I think it was to Boston, and saw them board the ship. There he stood, and he bade farewell to them. He stood on the quayside watching the ship going out to sea until at last it disappeared over the horizon, and he went home. Later he received a cable with the news that the ship bearing Mrs. Spafford and the girls had collided with another ship in the mid-Atlantic, and in just a few moments she had sunk. The four girls were drowned. Mrs. Spafford, almost by a miracle, was saved, put on another ship, and eventually landed in Cardiff, Wales. When she arrived, she sent her husband this cable: "Saved alone. What shall I do?"

Poor Mr. Spafford. Here is a Christian man, and he gets this tragic cable. Two years before that shipwreck, something else had happened to him. All his wealth was in real estate, but in 1871 there was a great fire in Chicago, the Great Chicago Fire, which destroyed much of the city. In one afternoon Mr. Spafford became a poor man. He lost everything in that fire—his money, home, his positions—and was reduced to poverty. And now he receives a cable telling him that he has lost his four darling daughters. How did he react? Did he say, "Well, I mustn't give in. I mustn't cry. I mustn't whimper. I must be courageous. I must brace myself. I must take it. I'm going to put up with it. I'll use all my powers to play the man in spite of everything"? Was that it? Dear me, no. This is what that Christian man did. He sat down and he wrote these words:

> When peace, like a river, attendeth my way,
> When sorrows like sea billows roll;
> Whatever my lot, thou has taught me to say,
> It is well, it is well, with my soul.

Do you see the difference? "When peace, like a river, attendeth my way." That is all right. We can all be happy on vacation. We can all say wonderful things when the sun is shining. But wait a minute. "When sorrows like sea billows roll" and rob me of my four dear daughters and everything, "Whatever my lot, thou has taught me to say, it is well, it is well, with my soul." Stoicism? No, no, a thousand times no! This is exultation. This is victory. He is more than a conqueror over everything that faces him.

This is exactly as we read in 2 Corinthians 4: "Our light affliction, which is but for a moment, worketh for us a far more exceeding and eternal weight of glory." This is Christianity. But what explains this? What made the apostle capable of using such language? It was simply that he was a Christian, not because he was the great apostle Paul. The grand story of the Christian church throughout the centuries is that thousands upon thousands of unknown Christians have been able to speak like this. You have never heard of them, but they were Christians, as Paul was a Christian.

What does that mean? It means that a Christian is a man or woman who has an entirely new view of the whole of life. How is this? It is through believing in the Lord Jesus Christ. There was a time when Paul could not speak like this. The problems and difficulties of life pressed upon him. He could not face them. But in Christ, everything changed. Paul will tell you in the next chapter of this epistle, "If any man be in Christ, he is a new creature: old things are passed away; behold, all things are become new" (2 Cor. 5:17). Not that they are changed, but Paul has changed, and he sees them in an entirely different manner. Everything is seen in the light of Christ. Henceforth he knows everybody and everything in terms of Christ. What has happened to him? Well, he is now in a new relationship to God. He knows God as his Father. He knows his sins are forgiven. He knows that nothing will be able to separate him from the love of God that is in Christ Jesus. He has believed the message concerning Jesus Christ and him crucified. That is the sole explanation. That is why he has an entirely new outlook, an entirely new view of the whole of life. And that is what the apostle expresses here in the two verses we are looking at.

The difficulty with us is that we are all so immersed in the petty problems of life that we do not see life as a whole. And what this Christian faith gives us is the capacity to see life steadily and to see it whole.[4] I sometimes like to think of the Christian faith as something that takes people up in an airplane or up to the top of a high mountain and enables them to view the whole landscape, the great panorama. Christians have a complete, a perfect, a whole view of life. "The world is too much with us."[5] That is our trouble. And we are beaten by it and defeated and immersed in it and lost. The Christian faith takes us up out of this world, and we look down upon it and see it from a different perspective. And here Paul explains just two respects in which this happens.

Notice how the apostle puts it: "Our light affliction, which is but for a moment." Now this is most important. One of the first great things that becoming a Christian does to men and women is to give them a right view of time: "but for a moment." And then in the next verse Paul says, "While we look not at the things which are seen, but at the things which are not seen: for the things which are seen are temporal; but the things which are not seen are eternal." Time! Most people today are being defeated by this time element. The problem of time is a great question, a great difficulty facing the modern world. And it immediately gets solved by this Christian faith. Let me show you in a very simple manner how this works.

It is time that defeats people. Take a man and his wife who suddenly lose their only child. All their affection and interest had been settled on this child, and, oh, how happy they were together! Suddenly their son is killed in a war or drowned in the sea. Someone who is dearer to them than life is suddenly taken away, and they are bereft. And this is what they say: "How can we go on? How can we bear it? How can we face it? Six months, oh, how terrible. A year. Ten years. Twenty years. It's impossible. How can we keep going? We've lost the thing that made life worth living." The tyranny of time. Time is so long. But Paul puts it like this: "Our light affliction, which is but for a moment."

Surely, you say, Paul was just a wishful thinker. This is just psychology, after all. How can he say "but for a moment" when life is long and arduous?

Ah, the answer is quite simple. The apostle, as a Christian, knows what to do with time. There is only one thing to do with time, and that is to take it and put it into the grand context of eternity. When you and I look forward, ten years seems a terribly long time. A hundred years? Impossible. A thousand? A million? We cannot envisage it. But try to think of endless time, millions upon millions upon millions of years. That is eternity. Take time and put it into that context. What is it? It is only a moment. If you look at time merely from the standpoint of your calendars and your almanacs and life as you know it in this world, it is an impossible tyranny. But put it into God's eternity and it is nothing. "What is your life?" says James. "It is even a vapour," a breath (James 4:14). You are here today, gone tomorrow. A moment! Christianity solves the problem of time. Christians are already seated "in heavenly places in Christ Jesus" (Eph. 2:6). They belong to eternity, and they are free from the tyranny of time.

But notice the second respect in which Christians have a different perspective: "our light affliction." When you first read Paul, he seems to be a mass of contradictions. He gives us this long list of his troubles, as we have seen: "troubled on every side . . . perplexed . . . persecuted . . . cast down . . . bearing about in the body the dying of the Lord Jesus" (2 Cor. 4:8–10). And then, having given us this terrible list, he looks at it and he says, "our light affliction." "*Light* affliction"? It is enough to crush a man. It is an awful weight. It is unbearable. It is enough to finish him. No, Paul says, it is "our light affliction." Surely, you say again, this is pure psychology, just wishful thinking. He does not face the facts. His whole list condemns him. He cannot possibly call this a light affliction. But wait a minute! Watch what he says. The apostle does not say these things are light in and of themselves. That is not what he says at all. What he says is that they become light when contrasted with something else. Listen to him: "For our light affliction, which is but for a moment, worketh for us a far more exceeding and eternal weight of glory."

The apostle Paul has a picture. Do you see it? Here he is with a table in front of him, and on the table is a balance, a pair of scales. There is a pan on one side and a pan on the other side, and he puts in one pan his toils, troubles, problems, and tribulations. And down goes the pan, with all that unbearable weight. But then he does a most amazing thing. He takes hold of what he calls "a far more exceeding and eternal weight of glory." The learned commentators will tell you that at this point Paul's language fails him. He piles superlative on top of superlative, and still he cannot say it. A "far more," an "exceeding," an exceedingly abundant "weight of glory." He puts that on the other side. What happens? Down goes the pan, and that first weight was nothing. He does not say that it was light in and of itself but that when you contrast it with this "far more exceeding and eternal weight of glory" on the other side it becomes nothing. Put fifty-six pounds on one side—it is a great weight. Put on a ton, and it is a great weight. Yes, but put the "far more exceeding and eternal weight of glory" on the other side and your ton becomes a feather.

What is the apostle Paul talking about? "Weight of glory." What does he mean? Oh, he has had a glimpse of the glory. He will tell you about it in the twelfth chapter of this epistle. He gives you glimpses of it in other places. What is a Christian? A Christian is a person who has been justified by faith and has peace with God, a person who stands in grace in Christ Jesus and rejoices in hope of the glory of God. The Christian is someone who has been given a glimpse of eternity.

You see, says Paul, I can only speak like this: "While we look not at the things which are seen, but at the things which are not seen: for the things which are seen are temporal; but the things which are not seen are eternal." Here is his secret. He sees into the glory by faith. And having seen that, everything else becomes light, almost trivial. Everything the world has to give means nothing to him now. He knows that all this can be lost in a second. If a hurricane comes, everything goes. In any case, death will put an end to it all. He does not live for that. "The things which are seen are temporal." Your homes, your cars, your wealth, everything can vanish in a flash. There will be nothing left. But as for these other things, "Eye hath not seen, nor ear heard, neither have entered into the heart of man, the things which God hath prepared for them that love him" (1 Cor. 2:9). Or, as Peter puts it, we have "an inheritance incorruptible, and undefiled, and that fadeth not away, reserved in heaven" by God for us (1 Pet. 1:4). Let your hurricanes come one after the other, and all together it will make no difference. Let men set off all their bombs in the whole universe at the same time, this inheritance remains solid, durable, everlasting, and eternal.

That is the secret. Once you have had a glimpse of this glory, nothing else can depress you, nothing else can alarm you, nothing else can get you down. "For our light affliction, which is but for a moment, worketh for us"—those afflictions make you look at "the things which are not seen." So they work *for* you. They drive you to this glory. They force you to consider it afresh. Far from getting me down, says Paul, they make me more sure of the glory of which I have had a glimpse—"a far more exceeding and eternal weight of glory." My dear friends, this has been the secret of the saints throughout the centuries. It is the secret of the saints today.

What do we know of this glory that awaits us? Listen to Paul putting it to the Colossians: "Set your affection on things above, not on things on the earth" (Col. 3:2). It is the same thing. The glory.

> The eternal glories gleam afar,
> To nerve my faint endeavor . . .
> For I am his, and he is mine,
> Forever and forever.

> JAMES GRINDLAY SMALL

My dear friends, orthodoxy is not enough, morality is not enough, experiences are not enough. The one question for each of us is this: Do we know something about this glory? Do we set our affections upon it? Do we live for it? Do we live in the light of it? Do we seek to know more about it? That is the secret of the Christian. It was in the first century, it has been in every century since, and it always will be until we finally arrive in the glory itself, changed perfectly into the image of our blessed Lord and Savior. "We shall see him as he is," and "we shall be like him" (1 John 3:2). May God produce in this evil age a body of men and women who can look at this life, which they share with everybody else at the present time, and, when everything goes against them to drive them to despair, can say, "For our light affliction, which is but for a moment, worketh for us a far more exceeding and eternal weight of glory."

2

THE GREAT WATERSHED

☼

But God hath revealed them unto us by his Spirit: for the Spirit searcheth all things, yea, the deep things of God.

1 CORINTHIANS 2:10

I want us to consider the second chapter in Paul's first epistle to the Corinthians. I would like to look at the whole chapter because, as I am hoping to show you, the apostle deals with one theme and one theme only in this chapter. Indeed, he keeps on repeating it in every single verse. It is a very modern theme. That is the marvelous thing about Scripture. It is always up-to-date, always contemporary. Here the great apostle deals with what, in many senses, is the most urgent problem and question confronting the Christian church at this moment. Let me put it like this: I think three things are characteristic of modern men and women that must amaze us and come as a problem to us.

The first is that amid all today's perplexities and problems, and they are truly stupendous and alarming—wars and possibilities of wars and the whole state of society in every country throughout the world—nevertheless, modern men and women, faced with such problems and baffled by them, refuse to consider the only solution to them—namely, the one that is to be found in the Bible. They will listen to statesmen or philosophers or poets. They will listen to anybody. But they will not listen to the message of this book, which alone can deal with their problems.

The second thing that is extraordinary about modern men and women is that they are hero worshippers. They are prepared to stand for hours to get just a passing glimpse of a movie star and will even stand in the rain in order to do so. They are always ready to turn someone into a hero. I am not here to criticize that. There is nothing wrong with hero worship per se. But what is astonishing is that people who are so interested in remarkable and unique personalities have such little interest in the greatest figure, the greatest personality this world has ever known, the Lord Jesus Christ.

The third thing that characterizes people today—and the three things, of course, belong together—is this: people are interested in great events, any remarkable happening. And yet when they are confronted by the greatest event that has ever happened or ever can happen, namely, the unique death of the Son of God on the cross on Calvary's hill, they pass by unconcerned or with contempt and derision.

Now it is really remarkable that people contradict themselves at these most vital points. The great question for us is to discover why this happens. And it is because that very problem is dealt with in 1 Corinthians 2 that I am calling your attention to it. Why do modern men and women not consider the message of the gospel? Why do they not believe it and accept it and apply it? I think the answer, quite simply, is this: their whole approach to this gospel is entirely and completely wrong. And because their initial approach is wrong, obviously they will be wrong with respect to the gospel in every single way and in every single detail.

Now the great apostle Paul deals with that very subject early on in this first epistle to the Corinthians. Paul had been to Corinth and had preached the gospel. Many had believed it, and a church had been established. But he hears, to his amazement, that many are now reverting to their old ways of thinking and are going back to human philosophy, human wisdom. This was one of the first reasons he had for writing to the church in Corinth, and he takes up this matter, immediately, in the first chapter. "Christ," he says, "sent me not to baptize, but to preach the gospel," but "not with wisdom of words, lest the cross of Christ should be made of none effect" (v. 17). And from there, really until the end of the fourth chapter, the apostle simply deals with this one great question. He is astonished at them. He points out that if they persist in this way, the cross will be of "none effect"; indeed, they are going to make everything that he preached to them of no effect. They do not realize this, but the Devil has come in, and in a very subtle way he is undermining their whole Christian position by getting these people to go back to their old style of thinking.

So in these four great chapters (1 Corinthians 1–4)—and it is because it is summed up so perfectly in the second chapter that I am dealing with this in particular—we have the apostle putting before us the essential contrast between the wisdom of God and the wisdom of man, the wisdom of this present world. And my suggestion is that so many today not only do not believe this gospel but reject it even without considering it, for the simple reason that they approach it in terms of human, earthly wisdom and fail to see from the very beginning that it does not belong to that realm at all but is altogether and entirely different.

Now this is such a vital matter that I do not apologize for taking you through it in detail. Let us start with human wisdom, "the wisdom of this world," as the apostle describes it (1 Cor. 2:6). For this, of course, is what is controlling the thinking of people today, and, alas, it is not only controlling the thinking of those who are outside the church but the thinking, it seems to me, of the vast majority of those who are inside the church. Here, I believe, is the great watershed that divides Christian people today. We are all on one side or the other. We either believe in God's wisdom and revelation or else we submit to the wisdom and philosophy of man.

Let us look at this human philosophy. You are all familiar with it. Human wisdom is always the same, though from age to age it assumes different forms. And the favorite at the present time is, of course, the scientific. This is what is controlling people's thinking. They look to the scientists. Scientists have become the new authority. People are prepared to listen to whatever a scientist says on any subject. Scientists have all knowledge, all understanding. The great characteristic of this age is that it is governed by a scientific outlook. And I want to show you that it is because of this that people reject the gospel and so deny themselves the results of this great salvation.

What are the characteristics of the scientific outlook, the scientific approach to all problems? We have been told so much about it on radio and television and in books that we are all familiar with it. The scientific outlook is an outlook that starts with man and his ability. It is all based on that. It believes that people have the power and the capacity to understand everything and to conquer their environment. How does this happen? Well, you start by observation. This is the scientific method. You observe. You look at the universe around you. Then, having made your observations, you collect your facts and put them together, you collate them. Then you look at them and examine them. And you discover that certain rules, or certain laws, are evidently in operation. For instance, you see that every year, with a strange regularity, you have spring, summer, autumn, winter. The scientist observes this, notes it, and sees that there is a law here that produces this cycle. One thing leads to another, cause and effect. And scientists also listen. They use their ears. They hear the sounds and collect them and coordinate them, collating them and proceeding to analyze them in the same way. And again, having done this, they arrive at a number of rules and laws, which are commonly called "the laws of nature."

But scientists do not stop at that. They now begin to reason about what they have discovered. And they say to themselves, "If this cause leads to that effect, surely that in turn might become a cause that will lead to another effect." And so they put up their hypotheses and say, "We'll try to see what happens when we turn this into a cause. Will it produce that effect?" So they make an experiment. This is the essence of the scientific method. You arrive at facts, and on those facts you build up a theory, and then you test your theory. You make an experiment; it is trial and error.

Take, for instance, the amazing things done by the great American nation in the twentieth century. For example, landing men on the surface of the moon. How did that happen? Well, to put it simply, scientists sent off a rocket, and it went up so high. They then said, "Now if we put another rocket into that first one and arrange that it should go off when the first one stops, more distance will be covered. Then if we put another one in that, it will go up even further." And on and on you go, until eventually you land a man on the moon. Of course, you do not always succeed the first time, but this is the method—trial and error, experimentation, verification or rejection of your theories. And at last you make your grand discovery, and you shout out your "Eureka!" That is the essence of the scientific method.

The scientific method is based on human ability—man's brain, man's understanding, man's power to experiment. It is based entirely on man's capacity, and it really believes that there is virtually nothing that is impossible to human beings. Some foolish men in England, I am sorry to say, men who have been in high positions even in the University of Cambridge, have the audacity to say that man is soon going to become the creator and God will no longer be necessary. Now modern people are controlled by that outlook. That determines their attitude toward everything. And that is why they reject the gospel. For here we have something that, as I want to show you, is the exact opposite of the approach I have just been describing to you. Let us note it together. I make no apology for taking you through every single verse in this second chapter of Paul's first epistle to the Corinthians.

Verse 1: "And I, brethren, when I came to you, came not with excellency of speech or of wisdom." Why did the apostle go to Corinth? Did he go to join the research team that was investigating truth or trying to discover reality? Was he a seeker and a searcher after the truth? No, no! Here is his word—"declaring unto you." It is the exact opposite. It is not seeking; it is declaring, it is pronouncing—"the testimony of God." Notice that the subject matter is entirely different.

Verses 2–3: "For I determined not to know any thing among you . . ." He knew many things. He was a learned, erudite man, this apostle, but he deliberately decided and determined to proclaim anything "save Jesus Christ, and him crucified. And I was with you in weakness, and in fear, and in much trembling." You will not get very far in the modern world if that is your condition, we are told! If you want to get on, you must be self-confident and assured. You must believe in yourself and in your powers. You must express yourself. But here is the exact opposite: "weakness . . . fear . . . much trembling."

Verses 4–5: "And my speech and my preaching"—watch the negatives—"was not with enticing words of man's wisdom, but . . ." What was it then? It was "in demonstration of the Spirit and of power"—why?—"that your faith should not stand in the wisdom of men, but in the power of God." Note the contrast. There is an antithesis in every single verse. It is not human wisdom; it is the power of God.

Verses 6–8: At first Paul appears to be contradicting himself when he continues, "Howbeit we speak wisdom among them that are perfect." But then, lest you think he is contradicting himself, he hastens to add, "yet not the wisdom of this world, nor of the princes of this world, that come to nought: but"—*but*, oh, the contrast, the absolute contrast—"we speak the wisdom of God in a mystery, even the hidden wisdom, which God ordained before the world unto our glory." It is altogether different. And then, to make absolutely certain that everybody has grasped this, Paul says, "which none of the princes of this world knew." Remember, when he says "princes," he is not thinking so much of members of royal houses or royal families as of the great men, the leaders in every realm and department of life—the great philosophers, the great thinkers, the great religious leaders, all of them. These are the princes who did not know God's wisdom.

Now the princes of this world are not to be despised. They are able men. And they are very able when it comes to recognizing one another. A great physicist recognizes another great physicist. A great philosopher recognizes another philosopher, a great scientist of any description recognizes a great scientist, a great poet recognizes a great poet, and so on. But the tragedy of the world is this: that none of the princes of this world knew him, "for had they known it, they would not have crucified the Lord of glory." Here is still the tragedy of the world. These great men, these able men who seemed to be able to do almost everything, did not even recognize the Son of God when they were confronted by him. They said, "Who is this fellow? Who is this carpenter? What's this nonsense about a redeeming death upon a cross?" None of the princes of this world knew him, and yet the Christians in Corinth were going back to the wisdom of these princes. And people are doing exactly the same thing today.

Verse 9: Then Paul adds a most amazing statement, as if he antici-pated the modern scientific method. "But as it is written, Eye hath not seen . . ." I told you that the first step, always, in the scientific method is observation. I was trained as a medical man, and I shall never for-get what we had drummed into us as medical students. Our teachers always used to tell us, "Now, don't rush at patients and begin to exam-ine them. Look at them first." Observation! It is the first rule in the sci-entific approach. But the apostle tells us here that it is no good. "Eye hath not seen." Man is very proud of his seeing, is he not? We are all proud of the giant telescopes that we have in different countries. They can penetrate so far. In England we have a marvelous telescope in a place called Jodrell Bank, and it can see immense distances. But con-cerning the truth of the gospel, our Jodrell Banks are useless. "Eye hath not seen," and never can see. Not only the eye, but the ear is equally useless. "Eye hath not seen, nor ear heard." Even your poetic imagina-tion is useless—"neither have entered into the heart of man, the things which God hath prepared for them that love him." The truth is entirely different. The things you rely on in the realm of science are already ruled out of court here. They are useless.

Verse 10: Then Paul caps it all off in this mighty statement: "But God hath revealed them unto us . . ." This is not about seeking and searching. It is not research. It is not trial and error . . . and error . . . and error. It is revelation—"by his Spirit: for the Spirit searcheth all things, yea, the deep things of God."

Verse 11: Then comes a great question for the modern man: "For what man knoweth the things of a man, save the spirit of man which is in him? even so the things of God knoweth no man, but the Spirit of God." What does that mean? Well, how does a man recognize a man? He is able to recognize another man because they have the same spirit. A dog can be a very intelligent animal, but a dog never really knows and understands a man. Why not? It is because a dog has the spirit of a dog, not the spirit of a man.

Before you can have true knowledge, there must be a correspon-dence of spirit. I can put this quite simply to you like this. There are many great scientists in the world, but they may get nothing out of poetry. There are many great poets in the world, but they may get nothing out of science. Why? Because if you do not have the poetic instinct or you do not have the scientific mentality, you are not able to understand the other realm. There must be a correspondence of spirit. "What man knoweth the things of a man, save the spirit of man which is in him? even so the things of God knoweth no man, but the Spirit of God." This is a basic statement, and yet this is what the modern world is incapable of seeing. Men and women believe they can arrive at any knowledge, every knowledge, but they cannot, by definition. As a dog can never really know a man, so a man can never know God in and of himself. The Spirit of God is essential.

Verse 12: And then, to make absolutely certain that we have all understood, Paul goes on, "Now we [Christians] have received, not the spirit of the world"—that is no good—"but the spirit which is of God; that we might know the things"—that we arrive at as the result of research? No—"that are freely given to us of God." You do not do anything about them. You just receive them in your utter helplessness. There is a complete antithesis in every sentence, in every verse, from beginning to end.

Verse 13: "Which things also we speak, not in the words which man's wisdom teacheth, but which the Holy Ghost teacheth; comparing spiritual things with spiritual." Is not the essential trouble in the Christian church today that people are even handling theology in terms of philosophy? They are going back to human wisdom, and they use great philosophical terms. They are speaking in the words that human wisdom teaches, but that is a denial of the truth, for this truth can only be expressed in the words "which the Holy Ghost teacheth; comparing spiritual things with spiritual."

Let me illustrate this. Imagine a man who has been trained in the classics, who is a poet by nature, trying to understand how men can be sent up to the moon; or picture him going into a laboratory and reading extraordinary scientific formulas. The poor poet! It is all gibberish to him. He does not understand it at all. He does not understand the language or the terminology. Or if you take your scientist, as I say, and give him the classics or a great bit of poetry, he may feel it is nonsense. And music may mean nothing to either of them. But this is the very confusion that is characterizing our modern world. People do not realize that you must compare spiritual things with spiritual.

Every discipline has its appropriate language. The scientist speaks in his scientific terminology. The poet speaks in his particular way. And these cannot be mixed. What would you think of a scientist, I wonder, who, anxious to propose to a certain young lady, sends her a list of scientific formulas? The idea is ridiculous. You do not express love in scientific jargon. You do it in words that convey love and that can be understood by the object of your love. But this is the whole essence of the modern confusion. People will handle spiritual things in scientific and philosophical terms, in terms of human wisdom. But spiritual understanding requires God's wisdom, and this wisdom can only be spoken in the words "which the Holy Ghost teacheth; comparing spiritual things with spiritual."

Verse 14: "But," the apostle says, to make his point abundantly clear, "the natural man receiveth not the things of the Spirit of God: for they are foolishness unto him: neither can he know them." There it is. It does not matter who he is—he cannot know them. Why not? ". . . because they are spiritually discerned." The type of Christian I can never understand is the Christian who is disturbed in his mind and spirit because these great scientists are not all Christians and some of them proclaim they are atheists. Some Christians are troubled that these great men with their great brains should not believe the Christian truth. My dear friend, you should not be surprised. "The natural man receiveth not the things of the Spirit of God: for they are foolishness unto him." They were foolishness in the first century; they are still so today. It does not matter how great we may be, nor how great our brains: if we are lacking the Spirit of God, we cannot understand the things of God and of necessity find them foolish. The modern scientist who denies the gospel is confirming the gospel.

Verse 15: "But he that is spiritual"—this man who is born again of the Spirit and has the Spirit in him—"judgeth [understands] all things, yet he himself is judged of no man." When people become Christians, they become a problem to their friends, who see the change and say, "What's wrong?" Their Christian friends are different. They believe things they used to ridicule. Of course! Christians are "judged of no man." That is because they now have spiritual understanding.

Verse 16: And then comes the close of Paul's argument. "For who hath known the mind of the Lord"—that is what we are talking about—"that he may instruct him?" And then comes one of the most astounding things the apostle ever wrote: "But we [Christian people] have the mind of Christ."

I think I have established my contention that in every verse in this chapter the apostle has been showing us the utter and complete contrast between the wisdom of the gospel (the wisdom of God) and every form of human wisdom. And here, as I say, is the whole tragedy of the world and of the church today. As they did in Corinth, so they are doing today. They are mixing these things up and causing unutterable confusion. Some reject the gospel altogether because of their human wisdom; others are turning the gospel into something that is of no effect. Even the cross becomes useless because it is expressed in terms of human wisdom as they try to understand it in their philosophies. This is the remarkable situation by which we are confronted today.

But why is the gospel, the message of salvation, essentially different from everything that belongs to the realm of human wisdom? Why is it that the two have nothing in common? The apostle gives us the answer in 1 Corinthians 2. It is because the gospel deals with a subject matter that is entirely and altogether different. And because the subject matter is different, the method must be different. I have shown you the scientific method. What is its subject matter? What is science concerned with? It is concerned with gadgets—radio, television, rockets. That is its realm. That is all right. I am not criticizing it. Those are the things with which human wisdom is competent to deal. Thank God for it, and all glory to these men and women and their great scientific achievements. That is the realm in which they are operating.

But what is the gospel of Jesus Christ about? Is it about scientific matters or politics? Of course not! As we have seen, the apostle tells us the subject matter of the gospel in the very first verse of this chapter: "And I, brethren, when I came to you, came not with excellency of speech or of wisdom, declaring unto you the testimony of God"—the attested truth concerning God. The subject matter of the gospel is the blessed Holy Trinity. Notice it in this chapter: God the Father; Jesus Christ, God the Son; and then the Holy Spirit: "God hath revealed them unto us by his Spirit" (v. 10). The gospel is not primarily about man but about God. It is a revelation of God, a revelation of the great mystery of God. And the apostle goes on to expound this and to unfold it. And the moment you realize this, you realize the utter uselessness of all human wisdom, even at its best and at its very highest.

"Canst thou by searching find out God?" (Job 11:7). Can a man ascend into that eternal realm where God dwells, God, "[who] is light, and in [whom] is no darkness at all" (1 John 1:5)? The thing is preposterous. God is Spirit. "No man hath seen God at any time" (John 1:18). It is impossible. And yet the modern man says, "I don't understand this. And because it doesn't conform to the rules of my scientific outlook, I'm going to reject it." Oh, what a fool the modern man is! What a baby he is, even in the realm of thought. Fancy bringing his abilities and his methods into a subject that, by definition, excludes it all! If people could understand God, they would be equal to God. God, by definition, is altogether "other." He is the absolute and the eternal, the everlasting God. That is the subject matter of the gospel.

And then the Son, the Lord Jesus Christ. "I determined not to know any thing among you, save Jesus Christ" (v. 2). And again Paul goes on to elaborate. He says, "We speak the wisdom of God in a mystery, even the hidden wisdom, which God ordained before the world unto our glory: which none of the princes of this world knew: for had they known it, they would not have crucified the Lord of glory" (vv. 7–8). What is the subject matter of our gospel, of our Christian message? It is Jesus of Nazareth. Who is he? Here is the mystery of mysteries, "the wisdom of God in a mystery." The world said of him, "This fellow" (Matt. 12:24; John 9:29). They dismissed him. The princes of this world did not know him. They looked at him and saw nothing in him but a man, and so they rejected him and regarded him as an impostor. But who is he? Here is my message, says Paul, and here is something that eludes the highest and the greatest human wisdom. This is the Lord of glory. "Had they known it, they would not have crucified the Lord of glory." This is the subject matter of Christianity—the mystery of Christ, God and man, two natures in one person, the incarnation. Here is our theme. It is so entirely different from everything that man is interested in and is competent to deal with.

Let me put this point to you in the words of Charles Wesley in one of his hymns. He puts it so perfectly. He seems to invite us to go with him to Bethlehem and to enter that stable and to look there at the little babe lying in a manger. I will look at him, says Charles Wesley. Who is he?

Oh, says the world, it's just a little baby lying in a manger. There's nothing to get excited about.

Wait a minute, says Charles Wesley:

Veiled in flesh the Godhead see;
Hail th' incarnate Deity.

Here is mystery. Here is paradox. The maker and the creator and the sustainer of the universe lying as a helpless babe in a manger. This is what we are talking about. What is the value of your scientific formulas here? Where is your philosophy? Where is all the wisdom of the scribes of this world? How utterly foolish it is, and how mad man is in his determination to unravel the mystery. The apostle Paul never said he understood it. He stands back one afternoon and says, "Great is the mystery of godliness: God was manifest in the flesh" (1 Tim. 3:16). That is it. It is entirely out of the realm of human wisdom in every single respect.

And then Paul tells us about the death on the cross: "Jesus Christ, and him crucified" (v. 2). Oh, the mystery and the marvel of the cross. Isaac Watts says:

When I survey the wondrous cross,
On which the Prince of glory died.

What a paradox, what a contradiction. The Prince of Glory dying? Madness! Impossible! But it has happened.

> My richest gain I count but loss,
> And pour contempt on all my pride.

The pride of knowledge and philosophy and all the learning that has been garnered in the universities says it is ridiculous—the Prince of glory dying. But this is the subject matter. The atoning sacrifice. God's way of redemption. "God was in Christ, reconciling the world unto himself" (2 Cor. 5:19).

And then Paul goes on to tell us that all this happened for us. This is "the wisdom of God in a mystery, even the hidden wisdom, which God ordained before the world unto our glory." All this happened that we might be redeemed. The Son of God died that we might be forgiven, that we might be reconciled unto him. And the Spirit is sent, and he comes and does his amazing work of regeneration. God puts his Spirit into us and gives us an understanding that we never had before. And so we have the mind of Christ. This is what the gospel is about. And the moment you realize the essential character of the subject matter of this gospel, you see how utterly monstrous and ridiculous and foolish it is for men and women to come with their wisdom and learning and understanding and apply it to this. They have already gone astray, and that is the whole tragedy of the world and the church at this moment.

My dear friend, we must make this perfectly clear. When you come into the Christian church and listen to this gospel as it is in truth, you must realize that everything you are in the world is of no value. It does not matter who you are, what your natural ability is, what your degrees and diplomas, your academic attainments, what knowledge you may have garnered. It is all useless to you. When you come into the realm of the church, the Pharisee is as helpless as the publican. The greatest sage is as helpless as a newborn babe. It is not only the apostle Paul who says this. Our blessed Lord said, "Verily, I say unto you, Except ye be converted, and become as little children, ye shall not enter into the kingdom of heaven" (Matt. 18:3). He said on another occasion, "I thank thee,

O Father, Lord of heaven and earth, because thou hast hid these things from the wise and prudent, and hast revealed them unto babes. Even so, Father: for so it seemed good in thy sight" (Matt. 11:25–26). And yet people depend on their human wisdom. The outsider does, and rejects the gospel. Even inside the church men and women bring their philosophy and their learning and their ability and make the cross of Christ of no effect through their human wisdom. That is the great problem in the church at this very moment. It is the failure to see this basic, elementary truth that the very character of the gospel makes it impossible for human wisdom ever to understand it or to be competent with respect to it.

What is the subject matter of the gospel? The apostle tells us in the tenth verse: "God hath revealed them unto us by his Spirit"—what is it?—"for the Spirit searcheth all things, yea, the deep things of God." It is the infinite depths of the wisdom of God. Let me again sum this up in great words by Charles Wesley. "'Tis mystery all"—and it is, from beginning to end—"th' Immortal dies." And then notice the boldness of Charles Wesley:

> Who can explore his strange design?
> In vain the firstborn seraph tries
> To sound the depth of love divine.
> 'Tis mercy all! [What has man to do about it?]
> Let earth adore;
> Let angel minds [all you seraphs and archangels] inquire no more.

You might as well give up, says Charles Wesley. You will never understand it. It is a mystery to you, this manifold wisdom of God, the deep things of God. So it is because of the subject matter of the gospel that human wisdom is utterly incompetent and should never enter into this realm.

I close by making this remark: is it not astonishing that men and women are annoyed by this instead of thanking God for it? We ought to thank God that the gospel is as it is. But people want to understand, do they not? They want to understand through their own minds and abilities. And in their utter folly they say, "If I don't understand it, I'm not going to believe it." Oh, this is the tragedy of humanity. Their ultimate trouble is intellectual pride and conceit. They glory in themselves instead of doing as Paul has told us to do at the end of the first chapter: "He that glorieth, let him glory in the Lord."

Why should we thank God that this gospel is as it is? Well, if it depended upon human wisdom and knowledge and capacity and understanding and power, then it would only be a salvation for a very few great and exceptional people. What if you did have to know philosophy and science in order to understand salvation and receive it? Then just a handful of people would be saved, and the rest of us would be irretrievably damned and lost. Thank God that his way of salvation is so utterly and entirely different from ours. Human wisdom and science postulate ability in our effort and seeking and searching and striving. But what does the gospel demand of us? Simply that we know that we are paupers, simply that we repent and admit and confess that we have nothing at all, that we are blind and lost and damned and hopeless and helpless. Oh, the tragedy that men and women should object to the most glorious thing about the gospel, that it is "the power of God unto salvation" (Rom. 1:16) and not the power of man. Because it is the power of God, there is hope for all of us.

Do you see how ridiculous the situation has become? So many today seem to think that unless you have great understanding and can read philosophy you cannot understand the gospel! If that were so, what would be the point of sending foreign missionaries to the heart of Africa or to the Australian Aborigines? What would be the point of sending people to preach the gospel to men and women who do not even know an alphabet and have never read a word in their lives and cannot follow any kind of argument or disputation? It would be useless. But that is not the gospel. The gospel is "the power of God unto salvation," and it is revealed by the Spirit. It is his power, not our understanding, that makes salvation possible. It is by the power that he gives to us that we are enabled to understand. The whole basis of the missionary enterprise is that this is the revelation of God and of the Spirit of God, that these things are freely given to us of God, and we but receive them in our utter, absolute helplessness and then proceed to understand them and enjoy them.

So the moment you begin to think about it, you see that human wisdom is an utter contradiction of the gospel in every single respect. And this is the final tragedy of the world. The apostle puts it like this: "We speak wisdom among them that are perfect: yet not the wisdom of this world, nor of the princes of this world, that come to nought" (v. 6). And this is what we must say to the world today. The world is proud of its wisdom, proud of its understanding, proud of its achievements, proud of its great scientific method. But do you know where all that will bring the world? The apostle has told us. It comes to *nought*. Nothing. A cipher. It appears to be wonderful, but in the end there will be emptiness, a void. Yet people hold on to their wisdom and reject this great and glorious gospel, which is the wisdom of God and "the power of God unto salvation to every one that believeth" (Rom. 1:16).

Why is it that men and women reject such a gospel? I am afraid the answer is but too plain and clear. It is because they feel that it insults them. They want to understand. They want to rely on their own abilities. And they hold on to these. And here they are with their world in flames, going to hell, and yet they still hold on. They will not submit. They will not come down. They say, "Any fool can do that." And they talk of their learning, of the advance of knowledge and of education. "We're asked to deny it all," they say. "We can't commit intellectual suicide." So they will not accept it. And their world goes on hurtling itself from disaster to disaster and will end in final doom. And all because of human pride.

Let me close by quoting to you that great hymn of Horatius Bonar in which he states it all so perfectly:

> I heard the voice of Jesus say,
> "Behold, I freely give
> The living water; thirsty one,
> Stoop down, and drink, and live."

Remember the invitation. Our Lord invites us to drink. Why does the world refuse? Well, the explanation is given in the last line:

> "Stoop down, and drink, and live."

"Stoop down"—that is the problem. Everything the world needs is there in the gospel. The fountain was opened on Calvary's hill. There is the water of the word of life. Everything you need. But you cannot drink from a fountain standing erect. Before you can drink, you have to bend on your knees, or you may lie prostrate on the ground. You must stoop down and drink in order to live. And the moment your parched lips touch that cooling stream everything is changed. But modern men and women will not do this. They prefer to stand and stagger on their feet in their inability and go to hell. If they would just become little children and stoop down and drink, they would be able to join Horatius Bonar in saying:

> I came to Jesus, and I drank
> Of that life-giving stream;
> My thirst was quenched, my soul revived,
> And now I live in him.

My dear friends, this is the great question of the hour. Are you banking and basing your whole position on human wisdom and understanding and knowledge or on the revelation of the wisdom of God in the Lord Jesus Christ, made known to us in the infallible Word of God? Oh, the tragedy, the folly of pitting human wisdom and understanding against "the deep things of God" (v. 10).

May God apply his message to us so that we all may know we are ready to be fools for Christ's sake. "If any man," says Paul in verse 18 of the next chapter, "seemeth to be wise in this world, let him become a fool" and believe this gospel. Let him become a little child that he may be made wise.

3

WHAT IS THE CHURCH?

☼

And they continued stedfastly in the apostles' doctrine and fellowship, and in breaking of bread, and in prayers.

ACTS 2:42

I should like to consider with you the second chapter of the book of Acts,
and in particular the forty-second verse, because here we are presented
with a picture of the early Christian church. In other words, I want us
to look at the nature of the church, the doctrine of the church. I do this
because I believe there is an urgent need to consider this subject at this
present time.

There are many compelling reasons for studying this doctrine. One,
of course, and a very big one, is what is called the ecumenical movement, with all its talk and activity in connection with the formation of
a great world church. This has occupied attention ever since the end of
the last war,[6] and even before the war, but particularly after 1945 and
the first gathering of the World Council of Churches in Amsterdam in
1948. Since then much of the time and energy of the church has been
given to discussing and preaching on the subject of church unity, ecumenicity, and so on. But it does seem to me that before we start talking
about uniting churches, we ought to be clear in our minds as to what a
church is, because so much of the confusion today arises from our failure to start with a doctrine of the church.

Another good reason for considering the doctrine of the church is
that this doctrine should come first in connection with the whole problem of evangelism. The unit of evangelism in the New Testament was
the church, and that has been the case throughout the centuries. But

there is a tendency today to think of evangelism in terms that do not include the local church, and I think this has been very detrimental to the true life of the church. So if we are concerned about evangelism, we must consider this doctrine.

Furthermore, when we turn to what is undoubtedly the greatest need of all in the Christian church today—the need of revival—the doctrine of the church becomes quite crucial because surely the Holy Spirit will not and cannot honor anything except his own truth. And if the church is uncertain about that truth, there will be very little value and very little power in her prayers.

All these are obvious, practical reasons why we should be considering together the doctrine of the nature of the Christian church. But over and above all these considerations is the fact that the New Testament itself gives such great prominence to this doctrine. There is a sense in which it is true to say that every single New Testament epistle is really concerned with it. Most of the difficulties that arose in the early church were due to the failure on the part of the people to realize this particular doctrine. Take, for instance, the first epistle to the Corinthians. This is what you may call an omnibus letter, a letter in which the apostle Paul deals with a variety of problems that have arisen in the church. But in essence he says that there is only one cause for all the problems, and that is that the people have failed to realize the nature of the church. Look at the first problem he addresses: the church is divided into groups and factions, which have formed themselves around the personalities of certain preachers. One person says, "I am of Paul," another "I [am] of Apollos," a third "I [am] of Cephas," and so on. What is the cause of that disunity? It is, says the apostle, that they have never understood that the church is the body of Christ. "Is Christ divided?" Paul asks. "Were ye baptized in the name of Paul?" (1 Cor. 1:12–13). They would be incapable of these factions if they realized the true nature of the church.

And then Paul goes on to deal with many other problems—the incestuous person, for example. And he deals with that problem in the same way. He says, "Know ye not that a little leaven leaveneth the whole lump?" (1 Cor. 5:6). The church is like a loaf or a mass of dough with leaven in it. And because that is the nature of the Christian church, if you get evil in it, that evil will permeate the whole of its life. Then the apostle talks of how the church members were quarreling with one another and even taking their quarrels to the public law courts, and he is astonished at this. He says in essence, you do not seem to realize what a church is. Why do you not appoint one of the lowliest members of the church to make a decision in these matters (1 Cor. 6:4)? When he goes on to deal with the questions of unconverted husbands or wives and the position of children, he uses the same argument.

And when Paul comes to the question of the more enlightened brethren, the stronger and the weaker brethren and the way they are quarreling, he deals with that, too, in exactly the same manner. Then you come to the next question, that of spiritual gifts, how Christians are vying with one another, some boasting of more spectacular gifts and despising others, and those with the lesser gifts feeling envious of those with the greater ones. There is terrible confusion in the church, and again the apostle deals with it in the same way. He says, "Ye are the body of Christ, and members in particular" (1 Cor. 12:27). The whole trouble is due to the fact that they have never realized the true nature of the Christian church.

Now Paul's exhortations to the church in Corinth are just one example from the New Testament. In all these epistles this great doctrine is taken up in the same way because it is absolutely crucial. And I have a feeling that somehow or another we have been neglecting this teaching. We have been talking about certain aspects without considering the vital doctrine itself.

The question is, how do we approach this doctrine of the nature of the church? And there are certain important negatives. One fatal method is just to start from where we are and to see what modifications or accommodations we can make in order somehow to arrive at a church. Now that is exactly what is being done by the ecumenical movement. It starts from the present position, and then it more or less asks the different sections of the church to make certain modifications, perhaps even compromises, in order to produce one great world church.

This is the kind of approach that is found in great businesses when for certain reasons they deem it wise to amalgamate. But that, I suggest, is a false way of facing the problem of the church.

I venture to suggest also that another false way is to go back into history. Many tend to do this at the present time. There is great value in history, and we can learn much from it. But there is a danger that if you merely go back to the origins of the different sections of the Christian church, you may end by hardening the positions—people will develop a denominational spirit that is inimical to true unity, and we shall be fighting for our own traditions. This has happened frequently. Nothing has been so pathetic and tragic in the history of the church as denominational fighting and quarreling, the jealousy and the envy—my church, my denomination, must be better than the one down the street, and so on. And many people are quite unaware of the real truth concerning their own denomination. They contend for their branch of the church because they belong to it. But why do they belong to it? Large numbers have no idea. It is simply an accident that their parents happened to belong to it, and they were brought up in it. But this is how carnality comes in, and even history can be abused by us in this particular way. We can learn from history, but we must not become slaves even to history. Tradition is good; traditionalism is very bad.

An even worse approach is one that, it seems to me, is creeping in very rapidly, and that is to take a kind of Gallup poll to find out what the people want. This has become quite prominent in recent years. The church asks: What do people actually want? What do they like? What do they think? And we pander to them. We say that people do not like much preaching, so we will preach shorter sermons. But they do like more of something else, so we give them more of that. The church allows the world and the pew, perhaps, to determine what is to be the truth.

Now all these approaches are surely quite wrong. There is only one thing to do as we face this issue, and that is to go back to the New Testament itself. It is here and here alone that we discover what the Christian church really is. There is this fatal tendency in all of us to turn that which is true into something that is false. I never shall forget, as long as I live, a phrase I once read in a little book on Protestantism written by the late Dean Inge, of all men, the Dean of St. Paul's Cathedral in London. I have forgotten everything in the book except the first sentence, and this is it: "Every institution tends to produce its opposite." And his whole thesis is that by now even Protestantism has become something that is almost a negation of itself. If you analyze the life and the history of the great denominations, you will find that this is true of practically all of them. They have become something that is almost the exact opposite of what their founders believed in and did. So it is our duty to go back to the New Testament itself. Let us go right back to the beginning.

This is most important at this moment. What is a church? What is *the* church? And the only authority on this question is that which we find in the New Testament. In particular, in the second chapter of the book of Acts we have the account of the origin of the Christian church. This is what the church is meant to be. This is what the church has always become in periods of reformation and of revival. It is commonplace to say that every period of true revival and reawakening is nothing but a return to the condition of the book of Acts. The only hope for the church is to get back to this, and the only hope for the world that is hurtling itself to hell is that the church should again become what she was in her origin. So I invite you to look at this picture with me.

What is a church? The first thing we must say is that it is a gathering of people. Why do I make such an obvious point? I make it because as I read some of the journals and some of the books and booklets that deal with this question, I almost get the impression that some people seem to think of the church not in terms of people at all. They seem to think of the church as something that is written on paper, as a confession on paper. Now I am not criticizing confessions. I believe in confessions. But a church, after all, is not a confession of faith.

I am referring to the argument that one so frequently hears from people who are concerned about the state of the church. They say, "Well, as long as my church holds to this confession, I'm going to stay in her." They do not seem to be concerned about the fact that more than half

SETTING OUR AFFECTIONS UPON GLORY

the people in the church, sometimes even up to 90 percent or more, no longer believe the confession. That does not seem to trouble them. The church has become a confession on paper. But, my dear friends, that is wrong. The church is a collection of *people*, a gathering of *people*. And this is quite basic and vital to our whole consideration. Therefore, we must look at these people as we see them in Acts 2, gathered together in the early church.

What was this gathering of people? The world has its gatherings—people often meet together in various ways. But there is something unique about this gathering that we read of in the second chapter of Acts. There is always something unique about the gathering of people who constitute a Christian church. Nothing else in the world is comparable to this. You can analyze all the meetings, you can understand them and explain them, but there is always something about the church that eludes us. There is something living, something vital, that no other kind of gathering is ever aware of. What is the great characteristic of these people? They gather together, but what brings them together? What is this unique factor that unites them? The answer is that they are people who have undergone a very great change.

Go back in your mind and imagination to the day of Pentecost in Jerusalem. An astonishing thing happened. The Holy Spirit descended upon those people in the upper room, and they began to speak in other tongues. They were filled with the Holy Spirit, and they became a phenomenon, and people gathered from everywhere to see them. Some thought they were drunk, "full of new wine" (Acts 2:13). But Peter got up and preached a great sermon. As he was preaching, something happened to some of those people who were listening, and they were the ones who were added to the original hundred and twenty and became the Christian church. This was the direct result of the preaching of the apostle under the power of the Holy Spirit.

So what did happen to the people listening to Peter? Well, the record tells us: "Now when they heard this [Peter's sermon], they were pricked in their heart, and said unto Peter and to the rest of the apostles, Men and brethren, what shall we do?" (Acts 2:37). The early church was a gathering of people who had undergone a profound change as a result of listening to apostolic preaching. Here in Acts the people have become aware of the fact that this message is speaking to them directly. These are not people who decided to join a church. They did not decide to take up religion. These are people who have been called of God: "For the promise is unto you, and to your children, and to all that are afar off, even as many as the LORD our God shall call" (Acts 2:39). The church is a gathering of people who are aware that God has called them.

What does that mean? Now this is not the occasion to go into the theology, but these people in Acts 2 are aware of what is known as *an effectual call.* They hear the message, yes, but they do not merely hear it; they hear it in a very personal sense. They realize that it is speaking to them directly. It is not something that they can listen to in a detached manner. It is speaking to their souls. It is making them think. It makes them see that they are wrong. They become troubled about their souls. They become concerned about their eternal future. They are "pricked in their heart" (Acts 2:37). They undergo conviction of sin.

My friend, you cannot be a Christian, you cannot be a member of the Christian church, unless you know something about conviction of sin. Do we all know this? Has there not been a tendency among us to take even into the membership of the Christian church people who know nothing whatsoever about conviction of sin? I say to my own shame, but to the glory of God, that I was received as a member of the Presbyterian Church of Wales without having any notion whatsoever of what a Christian was. I had never known any conviction of sin, and I was not even questioned about it. I was not aware that God had ever dealt with me. This is common, and that is why things are as they are. But these people listening to Peter have been convicted of their sin. They are in terrible trouble. They cry out in their agony, "Men and brethren, what shall we do?" (v. 37). They are aware that God the Holy Spirit is dealing with them, and they have been brought face-to-face with themselves. They see the enormity of their attitude to the Lord Jesus Christ, who has recently been ridiculed and condemned and put to death. They are in this agony of soul, and they cry out for help.

And Peter replies, "Repent, and be baptized every one of you in the name of Jesus Christ for the remission of sins" (v. 38). And they believe him. We know this because we are told, "Then they that gladly received his word were baptized" (v. 41). Not only are they convinced and convicted of their sin, but they repent. They acknowledge their guilt. They confess it to God. They believe this message concerning the Lord Jesus Christ, and they begin to rejoice in it and to feel happiness in it.

Now it is obvious that these people have undergone a profound change. They are not the people they were when they left their homes or their lodgings that morning to go and listen to these strange men to whom this amazing thing has happened. They have become different men and women. Something has happened to them that has made them new people, and so they join the church. For many, of course, this means they will be ostracized by their families, hated and reviled and persecuted. But that does not trouble them. Why not? Because of this great change that has taken place in them. They are separated from the world; they are separated unto the gospel and unto the church.

Then we are told, "And the Lord added to the church daily . . ." (v. 47). We have an idyllic, ideal picture here of a great unity of people. How do the believers manifest this new life that they have received? And the answer is that they do so by gathering together. Now that they have come to believe in that way, the church is the central thing in their lives. We are told that they "continued stedfastly" and "daily with one accord" (vv. 42, 46). These are the characteristics of the true members of the Christian church. They gather together daily, steadfastly, continuously. The truth about them is not that they attend the worship of the church once a year on Easter Sunday morning. It is not that they just attend now and again. It is not that they attend when somebody is seriously ill in the family or when there has been a death or when there is a wedding or a christening. No, no! They meet together constantly and regularly. We do not read that the apostles have to go around visiting them and reminding them that they have not been in church recently and they really must be true to their responsibilities as members and put in a more frequent appearance. They do not have to be whipped up and dragooned and wheedled, as it were, into coming to church. No, no! The difficulty with these early Christians is sending them home! They want to spend all their time in the church. They continue steadfastly, daily.

Why did the first believers gather together like this? Why did they come together day by day? Why could you not keep them, as it were, apart from one another? I do apologize, in a sense, for bringing in these negatives, but I am beginning to think that they are tremendously important. Let me point out that these first Christians did not come together to be entertained. Nothing to me is so pathetic about the state of the church today as the entertainment that has increasingly come into our services. There are churches that keep going by means of clubs and societies. I know churches—so-called churches—that keep themselves going by game nights and dances and dramas and various other human activities. That is not a church; that is a travesty of a church. That is the world. The world does such things, and it does them very well. But that is not what brought these people in the early church together. They did not come together to be entertained in any shape or form. So why did they come? The answer is given: "They continued stedfastly in the apostles' doctrine and fellowship, and in breaking of bread, and in prayers" (v. 42). And this is what we must emphasize.

The really significant point about the list in Acts 2:42 is the order in which these subjects are put before us. You notice that the first thing that is mentioned is *doctrine*, teaching—not fellowship. Now I emphasize this because the whole ecumenical movement is based upon the basic argument that fellowship comes first. People say, "Don't talk about doctrine. Doctrine always divides. We are facing communism and materialism and a sort of scientism, and we must all come together. It doesn't matter what we believe. It doesn't matter whether we agree or not. The great thing is that we should be together. All those who call themselves Christians are surely to be regarded as Christians." And so fellowship is put first. This is the thing to do: "We must work together, and then perhaps we'll begin to agree together." I need not waste your time with this. There is only one thing to say about it—it is a denial of what was true about the early church. Doctrine comes before fellowship, and unless our fellowship is based upon doctrine, it is not Christian fellowship. It is carnal fellowship. It is merely human fellowship.

Why must doctrine come first? There are many reasons. The first is that the early Christians came together because the Holy Spirit had dealt with them. He had convicted them of sin, as he alone can do. Their new condition was the result of the operation of the Holy Spirit, and the Holy Spirit is known as the Spirit of truth. "He shall not speak [out] of himself," says our blessed Lord (John 16:13). "He shall . . . bring all things to your remembrance, whatsoever I have said unto you" (John 14:26). He is the teacher. So the very being and person and nature of the Holy Spirit insists upon the fact that doctrine is absolutely basic. Not only that, salvation ultimately is the result of a knowledge of the truth. Remember how Paul put it to Timothy: "who will have all men to be saved, and to come unto *the knowledge of the truth*" (1 Tim. 2:4). So truth and teaching and doctrine must come into the first position.

Now let me enforce the primacy of doctrine by pointing out that it is only by putting truth first that you can save yourself and the whole church from error. Heresy was a problem that arose at once, even in the early church herself. Certain false teachers came along, and false teachers can be very nice, plausible people, and they insinuated themselves into the life of the early church. How do you test the truth of the teaching? How do you know whether something that is being said is right or wrong? It is absolutely essential that you should do so, and the only way is by having an external, objective standard of truth. You cannot tell the truth of a man's teaching by how good and nice he is. There are many nice and good people who are not Christians at all. Nor can you say that his teaching is right simply because he is zealous and very active. If you apply that test, what will you say when you find yourself one Saturday afternoon answering a knock at your front door and opening it to two young men trying to sell certain books to you? Jehovah's Witnesses are people like that. They are not at the baseball game or any other kind of game. In their zeal and enthusiasm they are giving their afternoon to going from house to house, suffering abuse and so on, in order to propagate their teaching. They are full of zeal.

The fact that people are zealous and enthusiastic does not guarantee the rightness of their teaching at all.

"Ah," you say, "but if a man has had some great and glorious and wonderful experience, it must mean that his truth is right."

No, no! I have already pointed out that the cults can give people experiences. Psychology can do the same. There is nothing so dangerous as to base the test of truth merely upon something subjective in men and women. There is only one way of safety. It is the truth as preached. It is the apostolic doctrine. Thank God we have it in a written form. We have our New Testament, and we do not judge people or movements subjectively. We apply the test of the Scripture. Does what we are being told conform to Scripture, the apostles' doctrine, the apostles' teaching? This must always come first. It is essential to the life and well-being of the church.

And so it has happened, in the long story of the church, that when there was a reformation or a great revival, the first thing that was always done was that a confession of faith was drawn up. The early church was driven to draw up her creeds because of false teaching. The Athanasian Creed, the Nicene Creed, the Apostles' Creed, and various others were not done for the sake of doing them. No, no! The whole life of the church was in jeopardy. The person of the Lord, the way of salvation, and other matters became such acute problems that the church had to meet together for the purpose, under the guidance of the Holy Spirit, of defining the truth over and against error and heresy. But today all this is not only unpopular, it is heartily disliked. It is even described by some as not being Christian at all. We are told we must not speak of heresy. We must not excommunicate anybody or exercise discipline. If a man has a loving spirit and is out to uplift his fellow men and women, he is a good Christian, it is said. But this is not only a denial of the New Testament—it is a denial of the most glorious epochs in the history of the Christian church.

In the sixteenth century, the moment the great Protestant Reformation broke in upon the church, its leaders began to form the great confessions—the Augsburg Confession, the First and Second Helvetic

Confessions, and the Belgic Confession. And it was the same in the Church of England with the Thirty-Nine Articles and, in the seventeenth century, the great Westminster Confession of Faith. The church in her great periods has always seen the absolute necessity of defining what she believes in order that wrong teaching and error and heresy might be corrected and driven out. That is why teaching or doctrine must always come before fellowship. There is nothing more dangerous to the true life of the church than reversing this order and putting fellowship before doctrine.

But lest someone might think that I am only preaching to ministers, let me show you that this is also true for the members of the church. For what we are told here is that *they*, these people, not the apostles, these people who were added to the church, *they* "continued stedfastly in the apostles' doctrine." Why were they so anxious to receive this? This is a great characteristic, always, of the true Christian, and we must examine ourselves by these facts. We are living in evil days. We are living in terrible days. There is only one hope for this world, and that is the church and her message. But you and I are the church. Are we aware of our responsibilities? Are we aware of the true nature of the church? This is no time for entertainment. The world is on fire. The world is going to hell. And the church must come back to this. You and I must come back to this. Do we conform to the picture that we have here in Acts 2? Are you as anxious to have this teaching as the early church was? They wanted the apostles' teaching every day. Do you?

Why did they want this teaching? It was because of the new nature that was in them. Look at that tiny babe. Look at any newborn animal. What does it do? The first sign of life is that it seeks milk. That is instinctive. That is how life always expresses itself. And new life in Christ Jesus always expresses itself in the desire, as Peter puts it, for "the sincere milk of the word, that ye may grow thereby" (1 Pet. 2:2). You must examine yourself. Do you have this desire for the Word of God?

Men and women no longer seem to have this taste for the Word of God. I am told that church services must only be about an hour, and that if the sermon is more than twenty minutes the minister is in trouble. My dear friend, you are condemning yourself. Are you tired of the preaching of this Word? Do you want it to be over as quickly as possible? Do you want more entertainment and less preaching? If so, you are just proclaiming that you are not like the members of the early church. You are not like the members of the church in any period of reformation or revival. Read the great story of even those groups before the Protestant Reformation—the Waldensians in northern Italy, the Brethren of the Common Life in Moravia and Bohemia and in parts of Holland. These men and women would meet in caves in order to be safe. What for? To study the Word of God and to pray about it. The same is true of the early Methodists and the beginning of all the great denominations. This is how they came into being. These people hungered and thirsted for the Word. They could never have too much of it. Is this true of us? This is the problem confronting the church, not whether or not to amalgamate some denominations. That will make no difference because they will all remain the same. But here is the vital question: are we as newborn babes desiring and thirsting for the Word, this sincere milk of the Word, that we may grow thereby?

But there is more. Look at it like this. These people in the early church had realized that their former position and way of life was due entirely to their ignorance. It was the preaching and the teaching of Peter's sermon that had enlightened them. And so they now saw that the greatest enemy of humanity is ignorance. They said, "We never knew we had souls. We never stopped to consider that. We never considered our true relationship to God. We never faced the fact of death and eternal judgment." But when they were awakened to their ignorance, they said, "We must acquaint ourselves with all this. We must have the knowledge and the information." And they said, "We can never get enough of this teaching. Let's have more and more."

But I will give you a still better reason why the first Christians continued steadfastly in the apostles' doctrine and wanted to hear more about these wonderful things. Having realized the truth about themselves, they realized from the preaching of Peter that there was still far more to be learned. Peter referred to Jesus Christ as "being delivered by the determinate counsel and foreknowledge of God" (Acts 2:23). He had introduced them to this great plan of salvation, this great scheme of redemption worked out by God before the very foundation of the world and now brought to pass. He had told the story of the Old Testament—the call of Abraham, the development of the message, and he had shown how finally, "When the fulness of the time was come, God sent forth his Son, made of a woman, made under the law" (Gal. 4:4). And then came the amazing fact of the cross and Jesus' death there—all these glorious truths. That was why "They continued stedfastly in the apostles' doctrine and fellowship, and in breaking of bread, and in prayers." Are you tired of hearing the message of the cross? Do you think you know all about it? Have you no need of further instruction? Do you not rejoice to hear about these things—the great plan in all its fullness and all its glorious coherence? Anyone who does not want more of this teaching has really, I would suggest, never understood the teaching at all. It is a sign of life—it is inevitable.

Another reason why they desired further teaching was that they were concerned about their relatives and their friends. They'd had this new experience. They were born again. They were new men in Christ. They knew their sins were forgiven. They were children of God. But their relatives, their friends, their loved ones were still in the old darkness and the old ignorance—how could they help them? What if they went to them and said, "Look here, I'm different. I've had a wonderful change. I wish you had it as well"?

"All right," some might say, "but a Christian Scientist said that to me, and a Mormon too. They said they've had marvelous experiences. So they would not listen to me."

If you really want to help your loved ones, these first Christians realized, you must know the truth. As Peter, this same man, put it later when he wrote his first epistle, "Be ready always to give an answer to every man that asketh you a reason of the hope that is in you" (1 Pet. 3:15). Can you explain the way of salvation to another? Can you give an account of why you are what you are? You cannot do that unless you have attended to the apostolic teaching. Without instruction you cannot do it. So this is essential if you want to help your loved ones and your friends. Indeed, it is a command. We are to "grow in grace, and in the knowledge of our Lord and Saviour Jesus Christ" (2 Pet. 3:18). Do you grow year by year? Look back ten years. Do you know more than you did? Have you grown in grace during the last ten years? This is the characteristic of the church, of the true members of the Christian church.

So you see that for all these reasons, teaching and doctrine must have the preeminence, the precedence, the priority. They must always come in the first position. The church is in this world as "the pillar and ground of the truth" (1 Tim. 3:15), holding it before men and women. "In the midst of a crooked and perverse nation," says Paul to the Philippians, ". . . ye shine as lights in the world; holding forth the word of life" (Phil. 2:15–16). And if ever that was true, it is true at this present time. The apostles' teaching is a very specific teaching. All the apostles taught the same thing. Even Paul, who came in later, was at pains to point out that what he preached was what the others preached also (1 Cor. 15:3). He came in as a kind of late arrival, as one born out of due time, but he had the same message. It is the universal message of the whole of the New Testament. There is nothing vague about it, nothing indefinite.

So we must put in the first position the desire for apostolic teaching and doctrine. And then, and then only, and on the basis of that, comes *fellowship.* And of course the fellowship follows of necessity. We say, do we not, that birds of a feather flock together. Of course they do. Like people are attracted by like, and they like to be together. "We know that we have passed from death unto life," says John, "because we love the brethren" (1 John 3:14), because we would sooner be with the people of God than with the greatest people in the universe who are not Christians. Why? Because we are sharers together of the same life. We belong together. We belong to the same family. We have the same nature in us. We are "partakers of the divine nature," as Peter puts it (2 Pet. 1:4).

But not only that. We have certain things in common. We have undergone the same experience. We realized we were sinners—hopeless, helpless, damned sinners—and that we were saved by the grace of God alone. We have been born anew. We have new desires, and we all have the same desires. We share the same interests and the same hope—the hope of glory. And we are all serving the same great Lord and Master and following the one and only leader. That is why these first Christians continued in the fellowship. They liked being together. They liked to talk about these things.

This has always been characteristic of Christian people. We see it in the conversion of John Bunyan, the old tinker of Bedford, in the seventeenth century. John Bunyan tells us, in his account of it in *Grace Abounding*, that this was one of the things that helped him above everything else. He writes that he was under terrible conviction of sin for eighteen months and was almost being driven to despair, but one day he was standing in a street in Bedford and he happened to see "three or four poor women sitting at a door in the sun," knitting and talking together about the things of God. And they were enjoying themselves. They were having fellowship together as they shared their experience of the new birth and this knowledge that they had, and John Bunyan said, "That's what I want. Oh, that I could belong to them!" And he spoke to them, and they were able to help him. This is inevitable. The fellowship comes out of this common teaching and common experience.

Then comes *breaking of bread*. This means the communion of the Lord's Supper. The people in Acts liked to "shew the Lord's death till he come" (1 Cor. 11:26). They liked to remind themselves of how they owed everything to that. They did actually have communal meals as well. But they celebrated his death in the Communion. He commanded the church to do this, and they did it gladly, and they rejoiced in it together. They were "one bread," as Paul puts it in writing to the Corinthians (1 Cor. 10:17). And so they rejoiced in declaring his death until he comes.

They also continued *in prayers*. The old preachers always used to say that the way to test a church is to examine its prayer meeting. They said, "That's the powerhouse. The thermometer by which you can measure the warmth of the life of a church is the character of its prayer meeting." What are the prayer meetings like in our churches? Are they powerhouses? Do you meet with others to pray? Pray for what? Pray for your preacher. Pray for your pastor. Here is a man weak in the flesh, as we are reminded by the apostle Paul: "We have this treasure in earthen vessels" (2 Cor. 4:7). Do you pray regularly week by week that the Holy Spirit may come upon him? I have a fear that the members of our churches are beginning to think that only certain people can evangelize. They will prepare only for some special effort. But do you pray daily and week by week for your own minister? The Spirit can come upon him at any moment. Do you pray that he may do so? That is the only hope. We need revival. We need the Holy Spirit's power upon us. Nothing will avail until we get it. Are you praying for this?

These early Christians realized their need of God's strength. Peter, this man who had just been preaching, was only a fisherman. They knew that he needed strength, as they all did. They were confronted by enemies, and they knew that nothing but the power of God could authenticate the message and do this blessed work. So they spent their time not only listening to the teaching and in fellowship and in breaking of bread but in prayers. Christian people, do you realize your responsibility at this dread hour? We can all pray. We are all called to pray. Do we feel the burden? Are we conscious of this anxiety? It is not enough just to bemoan the evil state of the church and to condemn poor unfortunate young people and others who are outside. That is not going to save anybody. Only one thing will save, and that is the power that came upon Peter and the others on the day of Pentecost coming upon us again, and then we will know blessed revival, Holy Spirit power, and the Word will go out with an energy and force that is irresistible. But prayers are necessary.

That, then, is the character of the early church. But I must mention one other thing. At the end of the passage we are told this about these people: "And they, continuing daily with one accord in the temple, and breaking bread from house to house, did eat their meat *with gladness and singleness of heart*, praising God, and having favour with all the people." And the result of that was: "And the Lord added to the church daily such as should be saved."

I am emphasizing the joy and the gladness. Is it evident among us? Why are the masses of the people outside the Christian church? Why

63

is the church, the preaching of the gospel, so ineffective at the present time? I think I can tell you. Indeed, those who are outside will tell you. They call us "miserable Christians." They say they do not come to us because they do not want to be miserable. We give the impression, so many of us, that we go to church largely out of duty, perhaps because we promised a saintly father or mother that we would go. But we often seem very reluctant. If we go once on Sunday, we think we deserve a medal, we are making a great sacrifice. We give people the impression that the practice of our faith is against the grain. It is not surprising that the people are outside.

Do you know what will bring people inside? It is when you and I are filled with this joy and gladness. It is an evil world that we are living in, and the pleasure mania and the drug taking and so on are simply a confession that men and women are afraid to face life. They are defeated. They are hopeless. And if we give the impression that we are sad and glum and that going to church is a matter of tradition or duty, they will pay no attention to us. But when they see that we are men and women who "rejoice with joy unspeakable and full of glory" (1 Pet. 1:8), when they see that, living in the same world they are in, we have something in us that fills us with a thrill and an exultation, they will rush to us. Let me give you a great example from history. It was something more or less like that joy in the early church that led to the conversion of John Wesley. Have you ever read the story of Wesley? He was crossing the Atlantic from England to come to America and in the mid-Atlantic a great storm blew up. It was so severe that all those on board were convinced that the poor little ship was going to go down. Now on that ship there was a small group of Moravian brethren, whom Wesley had been observing. When they met together and were having their prayers, they would sing their hymns, and they seemed to Wesley to be filled with an unusual spirit of joy. But now the terrible storm had come, and Wesley was alarmed. He was not ready to die. He was afraid and did not know what to do. He thought he would take a look at these Moravian brethren, and to his utter astonishment he saw that they remained unchanged. They were still filled with a spirit of joy and gladness and were rejoicing and singing hymns in the storm exactly as they had done in the calm.

This has always been the characteristic of the true church. And when she becomes like this, she acts as a magnet to those who are outside. When men and women see us with this spirit of joy and rejoicing, this spirit that is invincible, this spirit that knows God and is afraid of nothing, they will rush to listen to us. Joy and rejoicing! How much joy is there to be seen among us? How formal we are! How organized we are! How set we are! And the world is not interested. But when it sees this joy of the Lord in us, it will come and listen to us and ask us for the secret of this amazing experience that we are enjoying.

Lastly, they were *praising God* (v. 47). How much praise of God is there among us? I do not mean organized, artificial prayers. I mean a praising that wells up out of the heart as we thank God that he has ever looked upon us, the worst of sinners. Do we cry out with Charles Wesley:

> And can it be that I should gain
> An interest in the Saviour's blood?
> Died he for me, who caused his pain—
> For me, who him to death pursued?
> Amazing love! How can it be,
> That thou, my God, shouldst die for me?

It is amazing that he should ever have looked upon me. Yet he is "the Son of God, who loved me, and gave himself for me" (Gal. 2:20).

My dear friends, here is the great need of the hour. It is not merely that we should perpetuate a denomination or an organization or an institution. No, no! It is for Christians to become the living church of Christ, filled with his life and power, charged with the energy of the Spirit divine, and standing as a phenomenon in this modern, evil world. The world needs a church that points to the way of salvation and enables men and women to see that what has happened to us can likewise happen to them.

O may God have mercy upon us and awaken us out of our formalism and our lethargy and give us no rest or peace until we come to know him and rejoice and glory in him and are filled with his Spirit. "For the promise is unto you, and to your children, and to all that are afar off, even as many as the LORD our God shall call" (Acts 2:39). Let us make certain that we have been called—that each of us can say, "I know whom I have believed" (2 Tim. 1:12), that we live for him and, if needs be, we are ready to die for him, that in him we know we are always safe and secure.

O Lord our God, have mercy upon us, we humbly pray. We find ourselves so far removed from this picture of your people in the early church. O God, have mercy upon us. Come, we humbly pray, in the power of your blessed Spirit and awaken us. Convince us of our sin, and lead us to Jesus and his blood. Humble us, O Lord, and break us and bend us. Take from us our complacency, our self-satisfaction, and make of us a people who know their God, a people of whom he will not be ashamed to be called their God. O Lord, revive thy work. Make bare your own mighty arm, and do a new work in the midst of this evil and perverse generation in which we find ourselves. And unto you and unto you alone shall we give the praise, the honor, and the glory forever and ever. Amen.

4

THE CHURCH TODAY: THE ROAD TO EMMAUS

☼

Then he said unto them, O fools, and slow of heart to believe all that
the prophets have spoken: Ought not Christ to have suffered these
things, and to enter into his glory? And beginning at Moses and all
the prophets, he expounded unto them in all the scriptures the things
concerning himself.

LUKE 24:25–27

I would like to call your attention to a well-known incident in the life
of the early church, an incident that is described by Luke in chapter 24
of his Gospel. I want to look with you at the whole picture of the two
men taking the journey from Jerusalem down to Emmaus. It is very
important, as we consider this incident, that we should remember the
circumstances in which it occurred. We must remember that this happened after the resurrection of Jesus had taken place, and its whole sig-
nificance is really to be found in that fact. It is something that actually
happened, and it happened to two who belonged to the company who
had lived most intimately with our Lord.

As we look at these two men on the road to Emmaus, I am going
to invite you to look also at the state of the modern church. For here, it
seems to me, is an only too accurate portrayal of the condition of the
Christian church, speaking generally, at the present time. We were trying in our last study to consider the New Testament teaching concerning the doctrine of the church. Now we are going on to look at a picture
of the church in a state of discouragement, a state, indeed, of dejection
and perhaps even hopelessness.

I said in the previous study that there are many compelling reasons for studying the doctrine of the church, and one of the reasons that I gave was that those who are outside the church get their impression of Christianity and of the Lord Jesus Christ and, indeed, of God himself from what they see in us. It is not surprising that they should arrive at their assessments and their judgments in that way. We are the people who make these great claims. We claim to be the people of God. We claim to be "partakers of the divine nature" (2 Pet. 1:4). We claim to be special and unique, people who have an answer to the great problems of life. So they very naturally look at us, and they judge all we stand for and all we claim to believe by what they see in us. And I think there can be very little dispute that it is because of what they see in us that so many are outside the Christian church at the present time.

Now I know there are many who, looking at the state of the church today, feel that the one thing for us to do is immediately to consider what methods we can employ in order to win outsiders. That is a perfectly right and good thing to think about. But they start with that. They say, "Here we are, and there are the people outside who are indifferent to the church," and immediately they begin to consider means and methods of interesting and attracting outsiders. And some of them seem to be prepared to go to almost any lengths and to borrow any measures conceivable from the world itself in order to do something to get hold of these people. Now while I am in entire agreement with evangelism and would be among the first to say that the primary task of the Christian church is evangelism, I do, nevertheless, suggest that when we start immediately to think of the methods, of what we can do, to attract those who are outside, we are starting at the wrong point.

I suggest rather that the first question we should ask is, why are those people outside? And I have already given my own answer to that question. Indeed it is the answer they themselves give. They are outside very largely because of what they see in us who are inside. So I suggest that the first question that ought to be engaging us is this: what is wrong with us? What can we do about ourselves in order that we may attract the world outside instead of repelling it? Surely this is the first step. Instead of assuming that all is more or less all right with us and considering means and methods of winning outsiders, we should be concerned about dealing with whatever it is in us that is repelling them. We must bring ourselves into such a condition that we become an attraction and create within them the desire to be among us and to share the things we enjoy. That is why all this is so important for us.

For some reason or other we seem to be giving the impression to the world outside that one of the main effects of becoming a Christian is to make one miserable and to create problems and difficulties. Let me put it to you in a very simple picture. Look at the people who want to attend some game or other on a Saturday afternoon. Watch them as they prepare to go to that event. They keep their eye on the clock. They are anxious to be there on time, in fact before anything starts. And watch them as they go there. They are all rushing. They want to see everything from beginning to end. So they hurry along with great enthusiasm. Then watch them and listen to them while the game is being played. You hear them shouting and see them smiling. You see them almost in a state of ecstasy. They are almost beyond themselves, they are so enjoying it and are so thrilled by it all. And when the game finishes, watch them as they go home. They are all talking with animation, one commenting on this and the other on that. They are smiling. They seem to have had a marvelous time, and it has occupied them for hours. That is the picture, is it not, of the world indulging in its pleasures and in the things in which it believes.

Now take a look at Christian people, church members. Sunday morning arrives. What is the picture? Well, they are rather doubtful about whether or not they really will get up to go to church. After all, they lead busy lives, and a man must have some rest sometime! They did not say that on Saturday, but this is how they feel on Sunday morning. Going to church really is a bit of a burden, and their hearts are not in it. But in the end they decide they will go. After all, it is a matter of duty. So they get up. Are they anxious to be at church before anything starts, and do they want to make sure they get the best seats so they won't miss anything? You know the answer! The people on Saturday afternoon had only one complaint, and that was that the game came to an end too quickly. Is it like that with Christian people when they come to church on Sunday? Do they complain that the service ends too quickly? And what is the congregation like during the service? Are they moved with enthusiasm? Are they alive and alert and watching and waiting and listening? And how do they sing and join in? Is it similar to what happened on Saturday afternoon? Then watch them as they go home. Do they give the impression that they have been doing something wonderful and amazing? That they have had the richest and the highest experience that it is ever possible to have in this world? Are they talking with enthusiasm to one another about some aspect of the glory of the gospel or something that was made clear in the preaching of the Word?

We are far too much like these two men on the way to Emmaus. And that is why I am calling your attention to this whole subject. It is not only the pulpit that matters; it is the individual Christian. We are living in days when it is ceasing to be the habit, or the thing to do, for people to attend a place of worship. People are talking already about "a religionless Christianity" or Christianity without the church. So we must meet this acute problem, and the question is, are we ready?

It is my contention that the main responsibility at the moment rests upon the individual church member. It does not matter how wonderful a preacher your church may have if nobody will come and listen to him. And, after all, the preacher will be judged by the character of the congregation. And when church members give the impression that going to church is depressing or against the grain, then it is not at all surprising that those who are outside are not interested and have no desire to come to listen to the preacher or to attend an act of worship. In other words, I believe that we must look seriously at this picture that is recorded for us in the last chapter of the Gospel of Luke.

Look at these two men. Remember, the resurrection has just happened. But here they are, walking in a dejected condition on the road to Emmaus. Now we know that our Lord has realized that these men are miserable because when he joins them he says to them, "What manner of communications are these that ye have one to another, as ye walk, and are sad?" (v. 17). How does he know they are sad? He has not heard what they are saying. The answer is that if you feel sad, you look it. The man who is sad is a man who takes a certain stance, and everything about him suggests misery, whereas the man who is happy and alert and joyful shows it by his whole demeanor. And I suggest that the Christian church gives a melancholy impression to the world today because she is in a state of melancholy.

It seems to me that the best approach, therefore, to this whole incident is to look at it in terms of the state of the hearts of these two men and then apply that to the state of the heart of the church today. And in this paragraph we are told three things: the first is that each man has a sad heart (v. 17); the second is that they are slow of heart (v. 25); but, thank God, the third thing is the burning heart (v. 32).

And here we have a summary of this whole message. The great need of the church today, in our sadness and in our slowness, is to discover the secret of the burning heart. This is something, of course, that has been true of the church many times before. The church seems to go through these various phases from time to time and from century to century. And you will find that the great periods in the history of the church—revival and reformation—are always characterized by this burning heart, the condition in which these men ended. And so I say again, the great need for us is to discover what we have to do in order that we may have this burning heart, for the moment the church gets this, the problem with evangelism and the problem of the outsider are both solved. The moment the church gets on fire, the world is interested. It is interested in the phenomenon. We were looking in the previous study at Acts 2. The moment those disciples in the upstairs room were filled with the Spirit, this fire of the Holy Spirit, everybody came rushing to look at them. And it has happened in the same way throughout the running centuries.

Let us look, then, at these two men walking along the road to Emmaus. Why are they sad? That is the first obvious question to ask. Let us make our own analysis, and then we can look at our Lord's analysis of them because, fortunately, he analyzed them as well and dealt with them. Let us start with our own analysis. Why are these men in this dejected condition on this particular afternoon on the resurrection day of all days? Here is the tragedy of the situation, that this was possible. What was the cause? Well, these men really give themselves away. This is what I read: "Two of them went that same day to a village called Emmaus, which was from Jerusalem about threescore furlongs." Now take notice: "And they talked together of all these things which had happened. And it came to pass, that, while they communed together and reasoned . . ." (vv. 13–15). This is the cause of the trouble. There they are, walking on the road to Emmaus. And what are they talking about? Not the resurrection. No: "all these things which had happened," the wonderful three years they have had with him. One remembers this sermon, and another remembers the other sermon, and then this miracle and that miracle. They go over the past history, and they talk of what has already taken place. And while they are doing this, they are unhappy and miserable and dejected.

Is this not a perfect picture of the church today? So often we just spend our time talking about the great days that once were, the things that some of us even remember. Those of us who are older are particularly prone to this trouble. We look to the past and talk about the past, and we begin to idealize it, and the more we do so, the more unhappy we become. Tradition is excellent, but when you live on it, and when you become depressed by it, you already have a wrong attitude toward it.

In addition to that we have the terms "communed" and "reasoned." The two disciples are trying to understand the position in which they think they are. This is what Cleopas says when our Lord comes and challenges them: "Art thou only a stranger in Jerusalem, and hast not known the things which are come to pass there in these days?" (v. 18).

And then we read:

And he said unto them, What things? And they said unto him, Concerning Jesus of Nazareth, which was a prophet mighty in deed and word before God and all the people: and how the chief priests and our rulers delivered him to be condemned to death, and have crucified him. But we trusted that it had been he which should have redeemed Israel. (vv. 19–21)

They are reminding themselves of this person, the Lord Jesus Christ, all his preaching and the extraordinary power that he manifested in his miracles. But, alas, he died in utter weakness, and his body was taken down and laid in a tomb. That is what they are talking about together, and they are reasoning about this—how to explain it, how to understand it, how it could have happened. But everything they say betrays a terrible fallacy.

Whenever I read this passage, I am always reminded of the annual assemblies of the great denominations. This is more or less exactly what they all do. Somebody comes forward and reads the statistics, and then they begin to reason together about those statistics, and they begin to consider the problems. They will probably end by setting up a commission to investigate the cause of their problems. We are experts on the problems and difficulties. We know all about communism. We know all about rationalism and this and that. We have reasoned together, and we make our comments. And the more we commune and reason and talk, the more depressed we become. Exactly like these men on the road to Emmaus.

But I think the ultimate explanation of these men is that they are so certain of the death of our Lord that they have forgotten all about the resurrection. They are looking so much at the fact that he was put to death and buried that they have become absolutely blind to everything else. Now this is a very extraordinary psychological condition, and I suggest to you that it is the condition of the church today. We are all looking so much at our problems and our difficulties that we have become blind to the solution. We are experts in our problems. Never has the church been so skilled in analyzing its difficulties. The books that come off the presses almost daily give expert analysis and diagnosis. But there is never any solution. We spend the whole time reasoning and communing and talking together concerning our difficulties, and this has a paralyzing effect. I shall never forget an incident that happened in my own ministry.

I remember preaching in my homeland of Wales one Sunday in the early 1930s. I was preaching in a country place at an afternoon and then an evening service. When I finished the service in the afternoon and had come down from the pulpit, two ministers came up to me. They had a request to make. They said, "We wonder whether you'll do us a kindness."

"If I can," I said, "I'll be happy to."

"Well," they said, "we think you can. There's a tragic case. It's the case of our local schoolmaster. He's a very fine man, and he was one of the best church workers in the district. But he's got into a very sad condition. He's given up all his church work. He just manages to keep going in his school. But as for church life and activity, he's become more or less useless."

"What's the matter with him?" I asked.

"Well," they said, "he's got into some kind of depressed condition. Complains of headaches and pains in his stomach and so on. Would you be good enough to see him?"

I promised I would. So after I had had my tea, this man, the schoolmaster, came to see me. I said to him, "You look depressed." He was like the men on the road to Emmaus. One glance at this man told me all about him. I saw the typical face and attitude of a man who is depressed and discouraged. I said, "Now tell me, what's the trouble?"

"Well," he said, "I get these headaches. I'm never free from them. I wake up with one in the morning, and I can't sleep too well either." He added that he also suffered from gastric pains and so on.

"Tell me," I said, "how long have you been like this?"

"Oh," he said, "it's been going on for years. As a matter of fact, it's been going on since 1915."

"I'm interested to hear this," I said. "How did it begin?"

He said, "Well, when the war broke out in 1914, I volunteered very early on and went into the navy. Eventually I was transferred to a submarine, which was sent to the Mediterranean. Now the part of the navy I belonged to was involved in the Gallipoli Campaign. I was there in this submarine in the Mediterranean during that campaign. One afternoon we were engaged in action. We were submerged in the sea, and we were all engaged in our duties when suddenly there was a most terrible thud and our submarine shook. We'd been hit by a mine, and down we sank to the bottom of the Mediterranean. You know, since then I've never been the same man."

"Well," I said, "please tell me the rest of your story."

"But," he said, "there's really nothing more to say. I'm just telling you that's how I've been ever since that happened to me in the Mediterranean."

"But, my dear friend," I said, "I really would be interested to know the remainder of the story."

"But I've told you the whole story."

This went on for some considerable time. It was a part of my treatment. I said again, "Now I really would like to know the whole story. Start at the beginning again." And he told me how he had volunteered, joined the navy, was posted to a submarine that went to the Mediterranean, and everything was all right until the afternoon they were engaged in the action, the sudden thud and the shaking. "Down we went to the bottom of the Mediterranean. And I have been like this ever since."

Again I said, "Tell me the rest of the story." And I took him over it step by step. We came to that dramatic afternoon—the thud, the shaking of the submarine.

"Down we went to the bottom of the Mediterranean."

"Go on!" I said.

"There's nothing more to be said."

I said, "Are you still at the bottom of the Mediterranean?" You see, physically he was not, but mentally he was. He had remained at the bottom of the Mediterranean ever since. So I went on to say to him, "That's your whole trouble. All your troubles are due to the fact that in your own mind you are still at the bottom of the Mediterranean. Why didn't you tell me that somehow or another you came up to the surface, that someone on another ship saw you, got hold of you and got you on board his ship, that you were treated there and eventually brought back to England and put into a hospital?" Then I got all the facts out of him. I said, "Why didn't you tell me all that? You stopped down at the bottom of the Mediterranean."

It was because this man was dammed up in his mind that he had suffered from this terrible depression during all those years. I am happy to be able to tell you that as the result of this explanation that man was perfectly restored. He resumed his duties in the church and within a year had applied for ordination in the Anglican Church in Wales.

Now I tell you this story simply in order to show you the condition of these men on the road to Emmaus. There they are: "We had thought . . . but, oh, what's the use of thinking? They tried him and condemned him unjustly. They crucified him. He died, and they buried him. And he's in the tomb." They are so certain of this that they have become oblivious of everything else and blind to everything else. And I have a fear, my dear friends, that that is the trouble with so many of us. We are so aware of the problems, so immersed in them, that we have forgotten all of the glory that is around us and have seen nothing but the problems that lead to this increasing dejection. That is my analysis of these men on the road to Emmaus.

But let us go on and look at our Lord's analysis of them. It is much more devastating. In verse 25 we read, "Then he said unto them"—when at last they give him a chance to say anything. They have been talking so much that for some time our Lord has not had an opportunity to open his mouth. He simply put the question, "What things?" (v. 19), and they poured it all out. "Jesus of Nazareth . . . the marvelous things he did . . . all our hopes . . . we thought he was the Messiah. But, ah . . ." and on and on and on. At last they finish the wretched, miserable story.

"Then he said unto them"—what?—"O fools . . ."

I say again that I have an awful feeling that is what our Lord is saying about us and to us today. "You fools!" What he means is that we are dullards, that we are simpletons, that we do not know how to think, that we allow ourselves to be governed by circumstances and accidents and change and the things that happen to us and the conditions in which we find ourselves. And instead of using our minds and our reason and our understanding and applying the truth we have received, we allow ourselves to end in this state of misery and dejection and discouragement. "What a terrible world this is!" Is that not true of us? Fools! Simpletons! Dullards!

This is said frequently in the New Testament. Writing in his first epistle to certain churches, to unknown people whose names we do not know, strangers scattered abroad in various countries who were having a horrible time and were enduring terrible persecution, the apostle Peter says—and it is one of the first things he tells them, "Gird up the loins of your mind" (1 Pet. 1:13).

The church must think. She must use her mind and her reason. The tragedy is that we constantly tend to fall back on other things in order somehow or another to relieve ourselves and to keep things going. We are sentimental. Sentimentality is very largely the trouble with the present church. We are very nice people, we members of the Christian church, but we are very foolish. And the first thing we must do is wake up and gird up the loins of our minds and think and understand the truth and begin to apply it to the situation in which we find ourselves, instead of giving way, instead of giving in, instead of just commiserating with one another. I am sometimes afraid that the church is dying of niceness. We are really good at praising one another, are we not, and saying that we are doing well. We have become a mutual admiration society, sympathizing and communing with one another, and thus being sentimental with one another. And the whole time the condition of the church degenerates from bad to worse. Fools! We must apply our understanding to the situation with which we are confronted. That is our Lord's first word to these disciples. It is alarming. It is surprising. But, alas, it is true.

And then our Lord goes on to the second word: "O fools, *and slow of heart*." Here again is a most interesting condition, not so much connected with the mind as with this other part of us. Surely we all know something about this. The word "heart" does not only mean the affections. It means, in a sense, one's general condition. And I know of nothing that is more dangerous in the Christian life than this condition of being slow of heart. What does it mean? You have experienced it, haven't you? There you are, seated in your home. You have been reading the newspaper; you are taking it in, and you are alive and alert. And then perhaps you take up a book, maybe a novel or a biography, and you are enjoying reading it. Then you suddenly feel an impulse to read the Scriptures. You have not read your Scriptures much lately, but this call arises within you. So you put down your book and pull out your Bible. You open it and begin to read a passage of Scripture, but immediately you feel tired. You yawn and realize that you have had a very heavy day. You think that really you are not in a fit condition to concentrate. Your mind wanders, and you cannot keep your attention on what you are reading. Then you try prayer. It is exactly the same. You cannot control your thoughts. You have nothing to say, or your imagination travels all over the world. A deadness, a lethargy, creeps over you. Have you not experienced this many times? That is what is meant by slowness of heart.

"O fools, and slow of heart." The devil afflicts us with this spiritual lethargy. He seems to inject some kind of jaundice into us that paralyzes us and makes us dull. And we cannot rouse ourselves. We can be animated in conversation with others, but we suddenly become speechless when we are confronted by God. We can read other things, but not the Scripture. This is slowness of heart. The Devil, as it were, is causing this poison to circulate in our spiritual system. All our faculties are paralyzed. That is one of the troubles with depression. It affects the whole person. It affects the muscles, and people become physically weak. They cannot think clearly and cannot do anything properly. Slowness of heart. Now this is something we must be conscious of. It is not enough to say, "Well, I don't feel like it now." I should ask myself, "Why don't I feel like it now?"

Slowness of heart is a condition that must be dealt with. We must stir ourselves up. We must rouse ourselves: not only gird up the loins of our minds, but "stir up the gift of God, which is in [us]" (2 Tim. 1:6). Slowness of heart was the great disease of Timothy. The young man was always complaining to the apostle Paul about his difficulties and his problems. And that is what the apostle tells him: Stir up the gift of God, which is in you. Rake the fire! Wake up! Get rid of this dullness, this slowness, this lethargy. Shake it off. "Away, thou sloth and melancholy," as Milton once put it.

So this is the second thing that our Lord says to these disciples. He is severe with them—of course he is. It is wrong that they should be in this condition. It is a disgrace and a scandal. It is a sin. It is a denial of our Lord and of all that is so true of him. So he deals with them with great severity. And it is this kind of severity that has generally preceded revival in the Christian church. Painful though it is, my friends, we must face it.

Then our Lord goes on to his next word, which is, of course, the really crucial issue: "O fools, and slow of heart *to believe all that the prophets have spoken.*" That is the emphasis: "*all* that the prophets have spoken." This is very significant. Our Lord is referring here to Moses and the prophets, as he does again later that same day when he says to the entire assembled company of believers, "These are the words which I spake unto you, while I was yet with you, that all things must be fulfilled, which were written in the law of Moses, and in the prophets, and in the psalms, concerning me" (Luke 24:44). The two men on the road to Emmaus are Jews. They have been brought up on their Jewish Scriptures; they are familiar with what the prophets have spoken. What is their trouble then? It is largely the very fact that they are Jews and, as Jews, believe certain things in the Scriptures.

Now the coming of the Messiah, the Deliverer, was the great hope of the Jews. This is taught way back in Genesis and throughout the entire Old Testament. It is taught by the great prophets in particular. It was this that thrilled the Jews, and they held on to it. Yes, but they had their own conception of what this Messiah would be like when he came. They tended to think of him as a great political deliverer and even a great military deliverer. Their idea of the kingdom of God was that it was external, material, a political, social kingdom. And their idea of the Messiah was that he would be a mighty personage commanding great armies, and he would lead them to victory. He would restore the Jews to the position they had once occupied in the days of the great King David. He was to come of the seed of David, and they were to be world conquerors. This was the essence of the teaching of the Torah as they saw it.

The followers of our Lord had believed that he was the Messiah. So when he was condemned and crucified in apparent utter weakness, and his dead body was taken down and put in a tomb, they were utterly bewildered, utterly disconsolate, utterly cast down. But this was because they had only believed certain things in their Scriptures. Like all the Jews, they had selected out of the Scriptures the things that suited them, the things that appealed to their national pride and national sentiment, the things that thrilled them, their idea of the Messiah. As our Lord pointed out to the two disciples on the road to Emmaus, their whole trouble was due to the fact that they had not believed "*all* that the prophets have spoken," for the prophets had made it perfectly plain and clear. "Ought not Christ to have suffered these things, and to enter into his glory?"(v. 26). The prophets had not only spoken about a great deliverer, but of one who was to be "brought as a lamb to the slaughter" (Isa. 53:7), of one who would cry out in agony, "My God, my God, why hast thou forsaken me?" (Ps. 22:1). The prophets had spoken about the very things that had taken place, but these two disciples had not listened to them. They had only concentrated on what appealed to them and what pleased them, and it was because of this wrong and false attitude to the Scriptures that they were in a state of utter dejection.

On the road to Emmaus our Lord expostulates with the two men and reprimands them. He says in effect, "You do not even apply your minds to your Scriptures. You are thinking sentimentally and partially. Why do you not take your minds and use them on the very Scriptures of which you boast? And what of all that I taught you when I was with you? What of all that I said to you?" All this the disciples did not really grasp. They were so fascinated, for the time being perhaps, by his personality that they never really understood when he told them that he was going to be taken by cruel men and crucified and put to death and then rise again. He told them several times, but they never got hold of it; so when it happened, they were utterly confounded and cast down in dejection and despair. They failed to take in *all* that the Scriptures had written.

Is this failure not the real explanation of the state of the Christian church today? Somewhere around the 1930s a devastating movement began in Germany. It was a rationalism that led to so-called "higher criticism." Higher criticism is man picking and choosing out of the Scriptures, believing what he likes and rejecting, or ignoring, the rest. It is man failing to submit himself completely and utterly to the whole of the Scriptures. And I believe this is one of the most urgent problems confronting us today. There are even evangelical people who no longer believe the first three chapters of the book of Genesis. They are not believing *all* the Scriptures. But until we come back to a belief in all the Scriptures we shall be in trouble because we are setting ourselves up as authorities, and we are not competent to deal with the problems that face us. If we pick and choose, and believe this and reject that, we will ultimately have no authority whatsoever. We are so anxious to please the modern scientists, the modern educated people, that we have lost our gospel.

The Bible is a unity. We must take it all. It not only teaches us salvation, but it teaches us creation. It tells us how God made the world and how he is eventually going to restore the whole cosmos. If you begin to pick and choose from the Scriptures, you will soon end in a state of dejection. This is what the Christian church has been doing for so long, and it is not surprising that things are as they are. Here is our Lord telling these men, and I believe he is saying it to us today, that we must submit to the Scriptures completely, entirely, whether we understand them or not. Whether we can reconcile everything or not, we must submit to it. We must say that we believe this is the Word of God and we believe everything it says. It is history. It is an account of the creation and the fall. All these events that are presented as facts we must accept as facts; otherwise we shall soon be doubting the fact of Christ himself and even the very being of God. Here is our Lord's own analysis. There is a unity in the Scripture that must never be broken. There is a wholeness and a completeness, and it is only as we submit to this that we can look to the real solution of our problems.

Now consider what happened next:

And they drew nigh unto the village, whither they went: and he made as though he would have gone further. But they constrained him, saying, Abide with us: for it is toward evening, and the day is far spent. And he went in to tarry with them. And it came to pass, as he sat at meat with them, he took bread, and blessed it, and brake, and gave to them. And their eyes were opened, and they knew him; and he vanished out of their sight. And they said one to another, Did not our heart burn within us, while he talked with us by the way, and while he opened to us the scriptures? And they rose up the same hour, and returned to Jerusalem, and found the eleven gathered together, and them that were with them, saying, The Lord is risen indeed, and hath appeared to Simon. And they told what things were done in the way, and how he was known of them in breaking of bread. (vv. 28–35)

What a transformation! Look at these two miserable men going down to Emmaus in their melancholic attitude, talking and reasoning and communing together—hopeless. Look at them going back. Look at them hurrying. Look at them rushing. Look at them addressing the others, filled with fire and enthusiasm and hope and glory and rejoicing. What has happened? The burning heart! And that is the question. How do you get the burning heart?

"Ah," says someone, "you know, you're really depressing us. The hearts of these men were burning because the Lord Jesus was with them and because they recognized him."

Is that it? That is not what the record says. And this, to me, is a very glorious thing. What made the hearts of these men burn? Well, they tell you themselves. When they talk to each other after the Lord has gone, they say, "Did not our heart burn within us, while he talked with us by the way, and while he opened to us the scriptures?" That is the significant and wonderful fact. It was not after they recognized him, after their eyes were opened, that their hearts began to burn. Their hearts were burning when they still regarded him as a stranger. It was as he was opening the Scriptures when they were walking together on the way. Thank God for this. I have known many a person, and I have felt it myself many times, I am ashamed to admit, who has said, "If only I could have seen the Lord Jesus with my natural eyes as the people did who were alive in his day. Oh, how different I would be! If only I could have seen him, it would have made all the difference." That is a very great fallacy. You do not need to have a vision. You do not need to see him with your natural eyes.

There is only one thing that is necessary for this burning heart, and it is this—that you look in the Scriptures. It was as our Lord opened the Scriptures, showing this amazing plan of God, this increasing revelation, that the men's hearts were burning. He took them right back to Moses, we are told (v. 27). You do not even need your New Testament to get a burning heart! You can get it from the Old Testament if you know how to read it. What did our Lord do? He took them back to Genesis 3:15 and told them about the promise that the seed of the woman would bruise the serpent's head. That was the first promise of the Deliverer, the Messiah, and already they began to feel better. Then he took them right through it all—the promise that was made to Noah, the promise that was made to Abraham. He took them all the way through and showed that even in the law of Moses, with the lamb, the burnt offerings, the sacrifices, they were all pointing forward. Yes, and there is a sacrifice. A death is involved. "Without shedding of blood is no remission [of sins]" (Heb. 9:22). And then on to the Psalms, and then the prophets, and all of them saying the same thing, all pointing to him. Yes, and not only, I say again, to him in his great power as the Deliverer but also as the Lamb led to the slaughter, as the burnt offering, as the sacrifice, as the one who was going to die that we might be forgiven. And then our Lord showed them from the Scriptures that he would rise again, conquering all his enemies, and would bring "life and immortality to light through the gospel" (2 Tim. 1:10). And it was as our Lord did that, explaining and expounding the Scriptures, that their hearts began to burn and their whole condition was transformed.

And, my dear friends, that is the position with us today.

> I ask no dream, no prophet ecstasies,
> No sudden rending of the veil of clay.
> No angel visitant, no opening skies;
> But take the dimness of my soul away.

GEORGE CROLY

That is all we need. Do not look for phenomena. Do not look for strange, amazing, semimagical somethings. Go to the Scriptures.

"Ah," you say, "but it was the Lord Jesus Christ who expounded

83

the Scriptures to the two disciples. And if he only did that with me, I believe that my heart would be burning. But he doesn't come to us like this now."

Wait a minute, my friend. Do not fall into the same mistake as Thomas. Poor Thomas, when he was told of the resurrection, said in essence, "I won't believe it. I don't believe it. I can't believe it. It's impossible." His actual words were, "Except I shall see in his hands the print of the nails, and put my finger into the print of the nails, and thrust my hand into his side, I will not believe" (John 20:25). Do you remember what our Lord said to him? "Thomas," he said, "because thou hast seen me, thou hast believed: blessed are they that have not seen, and yet have believed" (John 20:29). Our Lord's literal, physical presence is not necessary. He has sent another, the Comforter. He has sent the Holy Spirit, and he is the teacher. He is the expounder. He is the one who brings back to our remembrance all that was taught by the Lord himself and explains it and makes it clear. This is the secret of every saint who has ever lived. They have not seen the Lord, but they are able to say with the writer of the hymn:

> Jesus, these eyes have never seen,
> That radiant form of thine;
> The veil of sense hangs dark between
> Thy blessed face and mine.

But he was able to go on:

> I see thee not, I hear thee not,
> Yet art thou oft with me;
> And earth hath ne'er so dear a spot,
> As where I meet with thee.

RAY PALMER

The Lord has promised to manifest himself to his people. He has promised to make himself known to them. And they can meet with him, and they are ravished, and their hearts begin to burn as they do so. The Spirit mediates. He was sent to do this. And this, as I said at the beginning, has been the secret of every individual whom God has used in the long history of the church, and it has been the secret of the church as a whole in periods of revival and reformation.

Let me give you a notable, well-known example. It all turns on how to get rid of a dull, sad, slow heart and get a burning heart. See it in the case of John Wesley, a brilliant, erudite man, religious, moral, and zealous. Over two hundred years ago he gave up a wonderful post in the University of Oxford and crossed the Atlantic with all its hazards to preach to the poor natives in Savannah, Georgia. Yet he was a miserable man, a miserable failure, and he said that as he tried to preach to those poor natives, he felt he needed to be converted himself. Then he went back, in the same condition, to England and was a failure and would have died a failure but for one thing. You do not think of him as a failure. You think of him as a flaming evangelist. What made the difference? He has told us himself. The story is well-known.

On the evening of May 24, 1738, John Wesley went to a little meeting in Aldersgate Street in London. He went feeling utterly dejected, absolutely cast down. He felt that he was useless. He was doubting everything. It was a very small meeting, and there was not even a preacher. But a man read out of the preface of Luther's commentary on the epistle to the Romans. He was not even reading the commentary itself but simply the preface! So there was this little man reading, and John Wesley said that as he was listening, suddenly his heart was "strangely warmed." He said, "My heart began to burn within me. I knew that my sins, even my sins, were forgiven." The cold iceberg of a heart began to melt, and the fire came in, and the man became a flaming evangelist.

John the Baptist prophesied that when our Lord came he would baptize with the Holy Spirit and with fire. Where is the fire, my friends? The Spirit descended on the day of Pentecost, "[in] cloven tongues like as of fire" (Acts 2:3), the fire of God, the fire of Mount Carmel, the fire that gives energy and power to a preacher and to a people in their prayer and their witnessing, in everything; the fire that burns away the dross and the refuse and produces the pure gold of a sanctified person.

The burning heart is the one great need and necessity of every one of us. Do you have it? If you have not, realize why you have not.

You are a fool! You are not giving your time to this. You are spending your time with your television or your radio or your newspaper. Give time to the Scriptures. Bring your mind at its best. Discipline it. Read the Scriptures. Start in Genesis and go all the way through. But never read without praying for the Spirit to enlighten your eyes and to open them and to give you understanding. Ask for this blessed unction and anointing that alone can enable you to find Christ. Look for him, the living Christ, the resurrected Christ. Look for him everywhere in the Scriptures. We must not spend most of our time in analysis of the problems. Shame on us! Let us stop looking at our problems. Let us search for him in the Scriptures and find him and look at him and bask in the sunshine of his face until our cold hearts begin to burn. Then we will scarcely be able to contain ourselves in the joy and in the ecstasy that we shall experience.

May God have mercy upon us and give us this burning heart.

O Lord our God, we again come into your holy presence and humble our selves before you. Lord God, awaken us out of our intellectual laziness and lethargy, our slowness and dullness of heart and of spirit. O God, awaken us and arouse us, and warm our hearts by the flame of your Holy Spirit. Make of us a people who know that we belong to a risen and a victorious Lord who shall reign from pole to pole and conquer his every enemy. Hear us, O Lord, for his blessed name's sake. Amen.

5

"SO GREAT SALVATION"

> Therefore we ought to give the more earnest heed to the things which we have heard, lest at any time we should let them slip. For if the word spoken by angels was stedfast, and every transgression and disobedience received a just recompence of reward; how shall we escape, if we neglect so great salvation; which at the first began to be spoken by the Lord, and was confirmed unto us by them that heard him; God also bearing them witness, both with signs and wonders, and with divers miracles, and gifts of the Holy Ghost, according to his own will?

HEBREWS 2:1–4

Let us consider together the first four verses in the second chapter of the epistle to the Hebrews. I want, in particular, to call your attention to that great question which is put to us at the beginning of the third verse: "How shall we escape, if we neglect so great salvation?" Now here the author of this epistle is addressing his first word of exhortation to the Hebrew Christians to whom he is writing, and in doing so he at once reveals his entire object in writing the whole epistle. "We ought," he says, "to give the more earnest heed to the things which we have heard, lest at any time we should let them slip." Some authorities say a better translation would be, "lest we slip away from them." They say it is a picture of a ship tending to slip away from her moorings. Both translations come to the same thing. The trouble with these people was that they were tending to forget the things they had heard, to the extent that some of them were even looking back to their old Jewish religion. And so he calls them back to the message of the gospel, exhorting them to give more earnest heed to it and to be very careful never to drift away from this great and glorious message.

I am calling attention to these words in Hebrews 2 because, in the first place, many Christians need this same exhortation in this day and generation and, second, because you might not claim to be a Christian and are not a member of the Christian church and I want to give you good reasons for believing this gospel. Let me put it like this: Why should we go on with this business of the Christian church? Why should the Christian church continue? Many in the world today are saying that the church has become an anachronism, that we might as well shut the doors, and that it is almost an insult to modern people to ask them to consider the message of Jesus Christ. So let us remind ourselves of the reasons why we should go on preaching the gospel and doing this vital work that has been assigned to the Christian church. And in these verses we have the answer.

We invite the world to listen to us. Why do we do so? It is because we are preaching "so great salvation." This is our message. This is why we should hold on to it. This is why everybody else should listen to it and receive it. So let us look at this statement. Is the writer of this epistle justified in describing salvation in this way? What is the message of the Christian church? We can never ask this question too frequently, especially at the present time when there is a terrible confusion as to what the message of the Christian faith really is.

We are at once reminded that the Christian message is a message of *salvation*. It is deliverance, emancipation, healing, liberty, health, vigor, power. This is the character of the message that we have been given to proclaim. But notice that the writer is not content with merely describing it as "salvation." He describes it as "*so great* salvation," and, of course, he does that quite deliberately. These foolish Hebrew Christians had been tending to lose sight of this. Their whole trouble, really, was that they had not realized as they should have the greatness of this salvation. So he at once reminds them of it—that this salvation of ours in Christ Jesus is the greatest thing the world has ever known or ever can know. And it is to this aspect that I want to direct attention in particular.

Those who are familiar with their Scriptures know that the Bible itself, and the New Testament in particular, always describes salvation in these superlative terms. The very picture of it that is always given to us in the New Testament is of its greatness, its grandeur, its largeness. Take the apostle Paul, for instance, in the second chapter of his epistle to the Ephesians. Language seems almost to fail him. He talks about grace, but he is not content with that. He talks about "the exceeding riches" of God's grace in his kindness toward us (v. 7). Indeed, in the third chapter of that same epistle, the apostle refers to "the unsearchable riches of Christ" (v. 8) and to "the love of Christ, which passeth knowledge" (v. 19). In verse 20 he writes, "Unto him that is able to do exceeding abundantly above all that we [could ever] ask or think." And this language is characteristic not only of Paul, but of all the New Testament writers. No one can read the New Testament with eyes open in the spiritual sense without getting the impression that salvation is something tremendous and magnificent.

That way of describing and thinking of salvation is by no means confined to the New Testament. The really great hymns always do the same thing. Not all hymns are like that. Some are sentimental ditties mostly composed about the middle of the nineteenth century. But the great hymns always bring out this element of greatness. Take a man such as Isaac Watts. When he looks at the cross, this is what he says: "When I survey the wondrous cross . . . ." The cross is not something you can take a fleeting glance at. It is too big for that. When we look at the cross, we are like someone standing on top of a mountain and viewing some great panorama that stretches out almost endlessly. "When I survey the wondrous cross . . ." The bigness, you see, the greatness of it all. Or take Charles Wesley. This is how he puts it: "O for a thousand tongues to sing my great Redeemer's praise." What is the use of one tongue? What is the use of ten tongues? What is the use of a hundred tongues? "O for a thousand tongues." Wesley had caught a glimpse of the greatness, the vastness of this "so great salvation."

But this is not confined to the hymnbooks. When you turn to the realm of art, you must grant that some of the finest masterpieces in painting and sculpture have been inspired by this salvation, this gospel. They are but an attempt on the part of the artists to express this greatness. You find it in architecture. Look at those great cathedrals on the continent of Europe. Even the ruins are worth looking at. The men who put up those magnificent edifices with their great vaulted roofs were trying to give an impression of the bigness, the exalted character, the magnificence of the great salvation that was being preached in those buildings.

You find the same purpose in almost every other sphere. If you are interested in oratory and in eloquence—and that is not to be despised— you must agree that some of the most eloquent orations that have ever been delivered in this world have been delivered by preachers. Great preaching, great oratory and eloquence—the modern world knows little about this. Perhaps the greatest preacher that America has ever known was Samuel Davies, and he wrote a hymn that expresses exactly the same sentiment:

> Great God of wonders! All thy ways
> Are matchless, godlike and divine;
> But the fair glories of thy grace
> More wondrous and unrivaled shine.

And nobody can dispute this point when we come to the realm of music. Probably the greatest single piece of music that has ever been composed is Handel's *Messiah*. What a magnificent piece of work it is! But what produced it? What led Handel to write the *Messiah*? Fortunately for us, Handel himself has told us. He says that during that extremely short period of time in which he composed this great masterpiece, "I did feel as if I were lifted up into the heavens and did see something of the glory of the great God." That is the explanation of the "Hallelujah Chorus"—not musical genius, but that Handel had had a glimpse of the glory of the great God. It is all expressive of the greatness and the magnificence of this "so great salvation."

So I make no apology for putting a question to you before we go any further. Do you habitually think of your own salvation as the greatest and the most wonderful thing that has ever happened to you? I will ask a yet more serious question: do you give your neighbors the impression that you have found the most magnificent thing in the world? I have already said this, but it merits repetition. I have a terrible fear that many people are outside the Christian church because so many of us give them the impression that what we have is something very small, very narrow, very cramped and confined. We have not given them the impression that they are missing the most glorious thing in the entire universe.

That is what the writer to the Hebrews is claiming for the gospel. The whole trouble with those Hebrew Christians was that they had lost sight of this greatness, and so they were going back to something else. So here is the question: is the writer indulging in hyperbole, or is he justified in describing this salvation as "so great"? In what sense is it right to describe it in this way? I shall answer the question for you in the writer's own terms. It is his answer, not mine. I am simply expounding what he says.

The first answer is that salvation is great in its authorship, great in its origin, great in its genesis. We generally judge the greatness of any book in terms of the authorship. When you go to the public library to borrow a book, how do you decide which book to borrow? I suggest that you usually do so in terms of the author. The author establishes the value of the book. And that is quite right. This applies not only, of course, to books—it is equally true of art. Let me give you a simple illustration. I remember reading in our papers in London about five or six years ago of something that had happened the evening before in Sotheby's, one of our great auction rooms. A painting had been sold at auction for £136,000. Why such excitement about that? Paintings often fetch tremendous prices these days.

The story is this: the man who had sold that painting had bought it some years previously. One day he had been rummaging around in an antique shop, not looking for anything in particular, when he suddenly saw the painting in a corner. Something about it attracted his attention, and he pulled it out. It was covered with dust, but he dusted it off a bit and looked at it, and he liked it. So he asked how much it was, and he was told that its price was something under £100. He bought it and took it home. He cleaned it up, put it in a new frame, and hung it on the wall with his other paintings. A few years later a friend of his, who was a well-known artist, happened to call on him, and the first man proudly showed his friend his collection of paintings. When the artist came to this one, he said, "Wait a minute, do you know what you have here?"

"Well, no," said the man. "All I know is that I like it very much." And he told his friend the story of how he had bought it and how it constantly pleased him. He said he was never tired of looking at it.

"Well," said the artist, "unless I'm very greatly mistaken, this is a painting by El Greco, the great Spanish master." And he was so sure of it that they brought the biggest art experts down from London. They treated it with chemicals. They X-rayed it. They did all the things that are done today, and the experts were unanimous in saying that this was undoubtedly by El Greco. Do you see what happens? When nobody knew who had painted the picture, it was worth less than £100. When it was known that it was painted by El Greco, it was valued at £136,000 pounds. It is still the same painting. You estimate the value by the painter, by the author, by the one who has produced it.

That is exactly the argument that the author of the letter to the Hebrews is employing here. Listen: "How shall we escape, if we neglect so great salvation; which at the first began to be spoken by the Lord"—that is the Lord Jesus Christ—"and was confirmed unto us by them that heard him; God also bearing them witness"—that is, God the Father—"both with signs and wonders, and with divers miracles, and gifts of the Holy Ghost"—the third person in the blessed Holy Trinity. Why is this so great a salvation? Here is the first answer: it has been produced by the blessed Holy Trinity. That is why you and I should hold on to it. That is why we should ask the whole world to listen to it. Look at the world in its terrible trouble. They have listened to the speeches of statesmen. They have listened to the philosophers, the scientists, the sociologists, the educators. Yet the world goes from bad to worse. What is our challenge to the world? It is this: *Come to church and listen to what God has to say about it all. This not the word of men; this is the Word of God. Listen to it!*

This writer is so full of the greatness of this salvation that he cannot contain himself. He does not even trouble to open with the usual salutation as he writes his letter to these people. He bursts upon them with the message. And this is what he says: "God, who at sundry times and in divers manners spake in time past unto the fathers by the prophets, hath in these last days spoken unto us by his Son" (1:1–2). It is God speaking! This is the greatest word in the world. Here we read the explanation of the state of the modern world, the predicament of the individual and the whole of society. This is not man's diagnosis; it is God's diagnosis and God's remedy. It is the authorship that makes it so great. The Father, the Son, and the Holy Spirit cooperated together—the *economic Trinity*, to use the theological term—to produce this "so great salvation."

There is the first reason. And, indeed, that is enough. In many senses I might as well stop now. But we are all, like these Hebrews, dull of hearing, so I had better go on and give you further reasons why this salvation is "so great." But I repeat, that first reason ought to be enough and more than enough for us. It is the word of God and not human words.

The writer has a second reason. He says this is so great a salvation because it saves us from a great and a terrible calamity. "How shall we *escape*, if we neglect so great salvation?" You measure the greatness of the salvation by measuring the greatness of the calamity from which it saves us. We are familiar with calamities these days, are we not? But these are nothing compared with the calamity that faces the soul that does not accept and believe this gospel. "How shall we escape . . . ?" The calamity is terrible, terrifying. Let me bring out this point by again using a simple illustration.

How do you estimate the value of drugs that are prescribed by doctors? I suggest that you do so like this. Consider the drug known as aspirin, a really useful little drug. If you have a headache, take aspirin. Aches and pains, take aspirin. A wonderful drug. But it is cheap, is it not? You can buy many tablets of aspirin for very little money. Why? Because it only deals with aches and pains, headaches, and things like that. But other drugs are very expensive. These are wonderful drugs. Why? Because they can cure not only headaches and aches and pains but the most terrible diseases. I remember forty years ago, and even later, if a doctor diagnosed a disease like tuberculous meningitis, he might as well have sat down immediately and written out the death certificate. Why? Because tuberculous meningitis was invariably fatal. Nobody could cure it. Nothing could affect it in any way at all. But they have drugs now that can cure tuberculous meningitis. They are called miracle drugs, and they are highly expensive. Why? Because they can cure these deadly diseases. You arrive at an assessment of the value of the drug by considering the lethal character of the disease that it cures.

And that is the very principle that this writer is employing here. "How shall we escape, if we neglect so great salvation?" Did you notice how he brings it home? Listen to the argument of verse 2: "If the word spoken by angels was stedfast"—he is talking about the Mosaic law, the law that God gave to Moses through the mediation of angels—"and every transgression and disobedience received a just recompence of reward; how shall we escape . . . ?" The writer is saying that the law of God has outlined the calamity and has defined it for us. He talks about transgression and disobedience of the law and the punishment that God has already announced that he will put upon such transgression. "The soul that sinneth, it shall die," says the prophet Ezekiel (Ezek. 18:4, 20). "The wages of sin is death," says the apostle Paul (Rom. 6:23). The law has pronounced this. And this is the great message of the whole Old Testament, which these people knew in a superficial sense. "The law was our schoolmaster to bring us unto Christ" (Gal. 3:24). "[The law] was added because of transgressions" (Gal. 3:19), so that "sin by the commandment might become exceeding sinful" (Rom. 7:13) and so be brought to the light.

Now the law has described and shown sin and its punishment, but, says the writer of Hebrews, the gospel shows it even more clearly. But taking it even at the level of the law, this message is needed by the modern world. Why is the world in general not interested in the gospel of Christ? There is only one answer to that question. People have never seen their plight and predicament as they are without the gospel. They think that as long as they live in an affluent society, as long as they have plenty of money and can enjoy themselves, all is well. They never stop to think of death and the judgment beyond it. And so they are uninterested and see no need for the gospel. They never see the calamity, the awfulness, the last judgment, and an eternity of misery and wretchedness outside the life of God. But that is the destiny of men and women who die in their sin and without believing on the Lord Jesus Christ. The law has already established this. Our Lord repeated it. He said that he had come "to seek and to save that which was lost" (Luke 19:10). He and he alone can do it. Nothing else can save. And that is this writer's whole argument. The law itself seemed to be enough. But now Christ has come, and he is the only way of salvation. If you neglect this, oh, the terror, the awfulness of the calamity and the fate that awaits you!

There, then, is the second reason for regarding this as so great a salvation. Here is something that can save you from everlasting and eternal misery and wretchedness and deadness outside the life of God, from the most awful calamity and fate conceivable—it can save you even from that. But that is negative, and this author is concerned to put it positively as well. This is a great salvation not only because of the greatness of what it saves us *from*, but because of what it saves us *to*, what it saves us *for*. It is still greater when you notice that to which it brings us and what it gives us. And that is the subject matter of the remainder of Hebrews 2.

What does this gospel give us? Someone may say, "Why should I believe that gospel?" Well, listen to the answer. The first thing that it gives you is pardon and forgiveness of sins. Notice verse 17: "Wherefore in all things it behoved him to be made like unto his brethren, that he might be a merciful and faithful high priest in things pertaining to God, to make reconciliation for the sins of the people." Reconciliation! There is nothing in the whole world today as valuable as this. To be reconciled to God! To know that our sins are forgiven! The wealth of the universe cannot purchase this. There is nothing more valuable.

Let me tell you the story of a man who once came to see me in London. I had never met the man, but he had asked if he could come and see me. I noticed from the address on his notepaper that he was obviously prominent in the great city of London, in the financial world. I could not understand why he should want to see me, but when he eventually came, he told me that he was following the advice of his physician. He had been seeing this great doctor, who happened to be one of the royal physicians, and this doctor could do nothing for him. What was the matter with the man? Well, he had been suffering from insomnia and from a lot of pain in different parts of his body. He had been to his local doctor and to the specialists, and none of them had been able to do anything for him. He had actually taken a world cruise twice, but he was none the better; if anything, he was worse. He was now in such a bad state that he could not do his work properly.

What was the matter with the man? He told me what it was. Twenty years earlier, in order to make a lot of money quickly, he had done something that was dishonest. At the time it had not worried him at all; in fact, he had thought it rather clever. He had made a lot of money and had gone on enjoying it. All had been well until five years ago, fifteen years after he had done this thing, when suddenly it came back to him. He did not know why, but he began to think about it. Something had resurrected it, and he could not get rid of it. So he began to develop these physical symptoms, these functional conditions of the body. Nobody and nothing could help him. He had plenty of money. If it were only a question of paying for physicians or world tours, there would have been no problem. But he could not find peace—peace of conscience, peace of mind, peace of heart. He could not put his head on the pillow at night and go to sleep, the sleep of the innocent. That was his trouble—his annoying, condemning conscience. And all the money in the world and all the libraries of the universe could not help him.

But thank God, a little preacher could help him, because he could tell him of a way whereby he could know for certain that his sins were forgiven. He could tell him about the Son of God who had come down from heaven to earth to deal with this very problem. He could say, as Paul and Silas said to the Philippian jailer, "Believe on the Lord Jesus Christ, and thou shalt be saved" (Acts 16:31). If he but believed, he would know that his sins were forgiven, blotted out, and he would put his head on the pillow and go to sleep like a newborn babe.

Reconciliation. It is more precious than the whole universe. Even millionaires commit suicide. You cannot buy happiness. You cannot buy peace of conscience and of mind and of heart. Money will not enable you to face death triumphantly. There is only one way whereby that can happen, and it is through this "so great salvation." That is the first thing that salvation does, but that is only the first.

Having reconciled us to God and having given us pardon and forgiveness of our sins, the gospel then goes on to do something that is almost incredible. It actually makes us children of God. We are not merely introduced to God and enabled to speak to him, but God adopts us into his family. Notice the greatness of the statements in this chapter:

> For it became him, for whom are all things, and by whom are all things, in bringing many sons unto glory, to make the captain of their salvation perfect through sufferings. (v. 10)

Now listen to this:

> For both he that sanctifieth and they who are sanctified are all of one: for which cause he is not ashamed to call them brethren, saying, I will declare thy name unto my brethren, in the midst of the church will I sing praise unto thee. And again, I will put my trust in him. And again, Behold I and the children which God hath given me. (vv. 11–13)

But the amazing statement is this: "Both he that sanctifieth and they who are sanctified are all of one." What does this mean? Who is "he that sanctifieth"? The Lord Jesus Christ. Who are "they who are sanctified"? You and I who believe in him. We are "all of one," but one what? One nature! We are born again. We are born of the Spirit. We are "partakers of the divine nature" (2 Pet. 1:4). "For which cause [Christ] is not ashamed to call them brethren." My dear friends, that is why the author of this letter says, "so great salvation." You are not only pardoned and forgiven, but you are adopted into the royal family of heaven. You have become a child of God. You belong to the heavenly family.

There are people in London who want to mix with great people and who pay large sums of money in order to get an entrée into some exclusive club. There was a time when *the* thing to do was to be presented to the Queen, and it used to cost thousands of pounds. People would pay this amount of money just in order to have the privilege of shaking hands with the Queen of England. But after they had paid the thousands and after they had shaken hands with Her Majesty, they were still the same people. They were still commoners. They were not taken into the royal family. They were not adopted. But here is what the gospel offers you—and for nothing—that you will become a child of God. You become someone of whom it can be said that the Lord Jesus Christ is not ashamed to be called your brother. Oh, the greatness of this salvation! The dignity of the position into which it puts us!

And not only that. On the writer goes. While you are still left in this world, you are a child of God, but you must still fight the world and the flesh and the Devil. Temptations are powerful and hot and strong, and how can you deal with them? The great salvation has an answer: "For in that he himself hath suffered being tempted, he is able to succour them that are tempted" (v. 18). The Lord Jesus Christ not only dealt with the problem of the guilt of sin, he deals with the problem of the power of sin. And so, believing in him, in the heat of temptation you can turn to him and say:

> I need thee every hour;
> Stay thou nearby;
> Temptations lose their power
> When thou art nigh.

ANNIE SHERWOOD HAWKS

"Cleanse me from its guilt and power," says the hymn-writer Augustus Toplady. Our Lord does that. This is a part of the great salvation. He will be with you. He will lead you. He will guide you. He has said, "I will never leave thee, nor forsake thee" (Heb. 13:5). He will go with you through all the trials and the troubles and the calamities, all the way through your earthly course. These are some of the things that this "so great salvation" gives us, but it does not even stop at that.

In many ways the greatest thing of all is what the writer describes in verses 5–8: "For unto the angels hath he not put in subjection the world to come, whereof we speak," says the writer in verse 5, and then he goes on to quote the eighth psalm. Now in the King James Version the translation in verse 5 is unfortunate. The writer is saying that the world to come, of which he has spoken and of which his readers have heard in the preaching, is not being prepared and reserved for angels but for us. In the last verse of the first chapter, in dealing with angels, he has said, "Are they [the angels] not all ministering spirits, sent forth to minister for them who shall be heirs of salvation?" And ultimately the salvation is this world to come, of which he is speaking. What does this mean? This, to me, is the most glorious aspect of all in our great and glorious Christian faith.

We are living in such an uncertain world. We are here today; we may be gone tomorrow—consider not only hurricanes, not only tornadoes, but the bombs and all the horrible possibilities. How long is the world going to last? Nobody knows. But it is an insecure world. You cannot of a surety base anything on anything. Everything is shaking. And to me the most wonderful thing of all is that as children of God we already belong to the world to come. Our citizenship is in heaven. We are only strangers and pilgrims here, as we are told later on: "Here we have no continuing city, but we seek one to come" (Heb. 13:14). We are like Abraham. In Hebrews 11 we are told this about Abraham: "For he looked for a city which hath foundations, whose builder and maker [architect and artificer] is God [himself]" (v. 10). A city with foundations, not a city that can be suddenly demolished by a hurricane or by bombs or anything else, but the city of God that is eternal! The eternal city. And "the world to come, whereof we speak" (Heb. 2:5) is not being prepared for angels; it is being prepared for us! Or as Paul puts it in Romans 8: "if children, then heirs; heirs of God, and joint-heirs with Christ" (v. 17). And in 1 Corinthians 6: "Do ye not know that the saints shall judge the world? . . . Know ye not that we shall judge angels?" (vv. 2–3).

This glorious world which is to come is for us. We are given it and made heirs of it, all for nothing, by this so great and glorious salvation. It is the free gift of God's grace to us. That is what salvation saves you to. It saves you *from* hell; it saves you *for* this everlasting and eternal glory that we shall enjoy with Father, Son, and Holy Spirit and all the spirits of just men made perfect and angels and archangels and cherubim and all the heavenly host forever and forever. That is why it is so great a salvation, the greatest thing in the universe.

But I have not yet mentioned the greatest thing of all. I reserved

SETTING OUR AFFECTIONS UPON GLORY

this to the end. Salvation is great in its authorship, great in what it saves us from, great in what it saves us to. But if you really want to know its greatness, you must understand the way in which it has been made possible for us, how it came into being. And this is what the writer of Hebrews elaborates. The point of the whole epistle, in a sense, is just to show us the preeminence of the Lord Jesus Christ. And the writer does that here.

We are living in an age when people are very fond of drama. People no longer go to places of worship on Sunday night because they are at home watching television—the drama, the play. Wonderful! And then they talk to one another about what they have seen. And they go to their theaters and do the same thing. You hear one saying to another, "You know, it was most moving. There was a man there—a great man, came of a great family, acquired a great name and great wealth. Do you know, in order to help other people he pretended that he was a nobody! He dressed badly. He mixed with ordinary people. He suffered indignities, suffered even the lack of food. He did all this and endured this great self-abasement and sacrifice. There's nothing he wouldn't do for them." And the speaker gets eloquent: "I was weeping. I was moved to tears as I watched it. It was all so marvelous and so wonderful and so moving and so loving. There was only one thing wrong with the play—it was too short. It ended too soon. I wished it had gone on." Drama!

Are you interested in drama? Well, if you are, let me in a few sentences hold before you the greatest drama that the world ever has known or ever can know. It is all described here. What is it? Listen to this writer as he puts it in the ninth verse of chapter 2 of Hebrews: "We see Jesus"— it is a drama about someone called Jesus—"who was made a little lower than the angels for the suffering of death, crowned with glory and honour; that he by the grace of God should taste death for every man." But who is Jesus? Here is the great question. Who is Jesus? He has already been described in the third verse: "The Lord." Jesus the man, Jesus of Nazareth, the carpenter. Jesus, yes. But more than that, he is the Lord! Ah, the writer has already said it, has he not, in the opening verses of the first chapter. He cannot contain himself. He is amazed at these Hebrew

Christians. What? Turning back? Going back to the old Jewish religion? Why? You have not understood who Jesus is.

Listen: "God, who at sundry times and in divers manners spake in time past unto the fathers by the prophets . . ." The writer is not derogating from the greatness of the prophets. They were great men. All right. But put them by the side of this one and they are nobodies. ". . . hath in these last days spoken unto us by his Son . . ." Who is he? He is the one "whom he [God] hath appointed heir of all things, by whom also he made the worlds." So who is Jesus? ". . . who being the brightness of his glory, and the express image of his person, and upholding all things by the word of his power" (Heb. 1:1–3). This is who Jesus is. This is what he was from all eternity, "the express image" of God's person, the effulgence of God's eternal glory, the express image of it all. He is the one through whom all things are made and who sustains all things "by the word of his power." He created everything, even angels.

The rest of chapter 1 goes on to tell us more about the angels and to contrast them with the Son. The Lord Jesus is the author of life. And yet listen again to verse 9 of chapter 2: "We see Jesus"—this glorious, blessed person by whom the angels and everything else was made— "who was made a little lower than the angels"—that is the drama. The apostle Paul wrote to the Philippians, "Who, being in the form of God, thought it not robbery to be equal with God: but [humbled himself and] made himself of no reputation" (Phil. 2:6–7). The Lord of glory was born as a helpless babe. He who gave the law was "made of a woman, made under the law" (Gal. 4:4). Here is the drama—the incarnation, the drama of dramas, Jesus' divesting himself of the insignia of his eternal glory. He could not divest himself of the glory nor of the deity. He divested himself of the signs, the trappings, the external manifestations. He did that in order to take on human nature.

Now the writer of Hebrews goes into detail over this. Note how he puts it in verse 16: "For verily he took not on him the nature of angels; but he took on him the seed of Abraham." Translate it, if you like, as, "He did not stretch out a helping hand to angels but to the seed of Abraham." He did take upon himself human nature. He was truly man and still truly God. But he humbled himself, he made himself of no reputation, in order to do this. He not only became a man, but he also became a servant. Here is the drama.

God not only cannot tempt anybody, he cannot be tempted (James 1:13). But as this writer goes on to say, here is one who "himself hath suffered being tempted" (v. 18) and, as he puts it in verse 15 of chapter 4, "was in all points tempted like as we are, yet without sin." Try to conceive of this. This blessed, holy person, this "holy thing" (Luke 1:35) born of Mary, this one who had looked eternally into the eyes of his Father and to whom sin was utterly abhorrent, was literally tempted "in all points like as we are." He humbled himself to this.

But wait a minute. We have not finished. "We see Jesus, who was made a little lower than the angels." Why did he do all this? What is the meaning of the incarnation? Did he come merely to teach us or to give us an example? No, no. ". . . for the suffering of death . . . that he by the grace of God should taste death for every man" (Heb. 2:9). Drama? "From the highest throne of glory to the cross of deepest woe."[7] The author of life being put to death: this is the drama of dramas. Nothing is worth talking about side by side with this. From the very height of glory he not only came into the world but went to death, even the death of the cross, and he died, and they took down his body, and they laid it in a tomb. The author of life, the sustainer of the universe, was buried in a grave. But thank God, that was not the end. Here is the drama.

It starts in heaven. It comes down to earth. It goes down to the grave, to Hades, as it were. What then? "We see Jesus, who *was* made a little lower than the angels for the suffering of death, crowned with glory and honour." But he burst asunder the bands of death. He rose triumphant over the grave. He could not be held by death. He arose "and hath brought life and immortality to light through the gospel" (2 Tim. 1:10). He ascended, and he took his seat at the right hand of God. The writer of Hebrews has said it all in the third verse of the first chapter: "Who being the brightness of his glory, and the express image of his person, and upholding all things by the word of his power, when he had by himself purged our sins, sat down on the right hand of the Majesty on high."

And there he is now, having come from heaven, down to the depths and back again to the glory. And there he lives and reigns, and history is in his hands. He is but waiting "till his enemies be made his footstool" (Heb. 10:13). And he will come again, riding the clouds of heaven, surrounded by all the holy angels, to judge the world. In all the panoply of his eternal glory, in all the majesty of his glorious deity, he will come, and every eye shall see him. But those who believe in him will rise to be with him and will share in his glory and will enjoy his presence and the indescribable blessings of the eternal kingdom forever and forever.

My dear friends, he did all this so that you and I might be saved from the calamity of hell, that we might be reconciled to God, that we might become the children of God, that we might share glory with God throughout the countless ages of eternity. Great salvation! Is anything else worth talking about? Do you apologize for being a Christian? Do you attend the house of God grudgingly? Are you giving people the impression that you have something small and narrow? Shame on you! If that is so, it is simply because you have never seen the greatness of this "so great salvation."

Do we not all need that "eyesalve" about which the Lord himself spoke to the church at Laodicea (see Rev. 3:18)? You can get it for nothing. Pray for it. Pray that the Holy Spirit may enlighten the eyes of your understanding, that you may see this "so great salvation" and especially the Savior himself, the Lord of glory, who came down and endured such shame that you and I might live. The Son of God, as John Calvin put it, became the Son of Man so that the sinful sons of men might be made the sons of God. "So great salvation." What can we say as we look at it? There is only one thing to say.

> Crown him with many crowns,
> The Lamb upon his throne.
> Hark! How the heavenly anthem drowns
> All music but its own.
> Awake, my soul, and sing
> Of him who died for thee,
> And hail him as thy matchless King
> Through all eternity.

MATTHEW BRIDGES

Have you seen the greatness, the glory of it all? Give yourself no rest or peace until you find yourself lost in wonder, love, and praise at so great a salvation and especially as you look at him and fall at his feet and look forward to the day when you will cast your crown before him.

O Lord our God, we again beseech you to have mercy upon us—for our smallness, for our ignorance, for our folly, O God, but above all for the harm we do to the gospel with our small notions and ideas and our pettiness and our concern with small, immaterial things. Open our eyes, we humbly pray. Give us a glimpse of him, the Lord of glory, who so loved us that he gave himself for us. Open our eyes, O Lord our God, that we may ever live to the praise of the glory of your grace. We ask this in his most holy name. Amen.

6

EVANGELISM: A VERY MODERN PROBLEM

❋

For our gospel came not unto you in word only, but also in power, and in the Holy Ghost, and in much assurance.

1 THESSALONIANS 1:5

The key, as I want to show you, to the whole first chapter of Paul's first letter to the Thessalonians is found in verse 5. But I do not propose merely to deal with that statement. I also want to look at the entire passage because I want to try to show that in this chapter the great apostle deals with a modern problem, perhaps one of the most pressing and urgent problems confronting the Christian church at this present time. That problem is none other than that of evangelism. I know that it is not always referred to in those terms at the present time. We do not talk as much as we used to about evangelism. We feel that we are living in a different world, that people are different and that we are different. So we have our new terms, and now the problem is the problem of "communication." But, of course, this is just another instance of the way in which we fool ourselves by changing terms. It is really the same old problem, the problem of evangelism.

As we know, every section of the Christian church is very concerned about the problem of evangelism and has been trying to deal with it for many years. Many commissions have been set up. Many gatherings have been held. Many books have been written on the subject. There is a feeling that somehow or other the Christian church is failing to get her message over to the world that is outside. We believe that this message

SETTING OUR AFFECTIONS UPON GLORY

and this alone can deal with the problems of mankind. But the question is, how can we communicate this?

Another new term is *articulate*. How can we articulate the gospel? How exactly are we to do this? This is causing great concern because, we are told, we are living in a post-Christian era, we are living in the atomic age, the scientific age. And somehow the idea is that people are now altogether different, and it is no use doing what the church has done before and in the way she has done it throughout the centuries; we must have something new. For these reasons there must be some new way of evangelism and of communicating the gospel. And great effort and endeavor has gone into the attempt to discover how exactly we can do this.

Now some feel that we need a new message, a new gospel. They say, "It's no use asking modern people, with their scientific knowledge, to believe what their forefathers believed. It's no use asking them to believe in a three-tier universe. They know too much, scientifically, to be able to accept the miraculous and the supernatural and so on." There is a movement on the continent of Europe associated with a man named Rudolf Bultmann. This movement says that the greatest hindrance to the acceptance of the message of the New Testament is the fact that unfortunately there are accretions, additions, to the essential message—additions such as the virgin birth, miracles worked by our Lord and the apostles and others, and the whole idea of the supernatural. Bultmann teaches, and many on the continent of Europe follow him, that the thing we must do is to get rid of the supernatural and miraculous element. We must "demythologize" the gospel, we are told, before it can possibly be accepted by people today. Many others are propounding their theories and ideas also. These men say that what we need is a new message for this new age, for man come of age, for man grown up.

Another major school of thought says, "That isn't what's needed. It isn't so much a new message we need as new methods." These people concentrate entirely on the question of methods. They say, "How does big business succeed? How does any enterprise succeed in the world?"

And they look around and discover that success is achieved as the result of advertising. You need a little money to advertise, so they persuade people to give it. They present themselves and promote themselves, and an advertising agency comes into being. And then they say that secular agencies use certain instruments—television, radio, and so on—and these agencies understand the psychology of the people, the psychology of salesmanship; so the church must become interested in these things. She has a commodity to sell, as it were, a message to give to the people, and she must learn from big business and from the advertising people. This is how to achieve success.

A great deal of attention has been paid to this question of method. Particular types of services are planned almost down to the last minute, and in these services everything is designed to appeal to the palates of modern people. It is argued that as long as we adopt these new methods, the people will come and listen to us, and the gospel will be propagated and will begin to influence their lives. Now it is important that we should be aware of exactly what is happening. The argument is that if we apply one or the other of these methods, and perhaps both together, then the church has some hope of getting her message over to this post-Christian world, to this atomic age.

I shall not weary you by analyzing those theories in detail. My whole position is simply that all this is entirely wrong because it is based on the assumption that we are faced with a new position, and that is something that I cannot grant even for a moment. There is nothing new about the problem confronting the church. The church has always had this problem, and that is why I am calling your attention to this particular chapter in Paul's first epistle to the Thessalonians, for here is an account by the apostle Paul of how the gospel was propagated and how churches came into being in the first century. This letter is said by the scholars to be the apostle's first epistle, and that is interesting in and of itself. In this first chapter Paul reminds these members of the church in Thessalonica of how the gospel came to them and how they had become a church.

I want to show you, and it is very simple to do, that when the apostle went to Thessalonica, he was confronted by precisely the same problem that confronts us at this present time. And that is why I am saying that instead of wasting our time trying to discover a new message or how to apply methods used by the world to bring success, all we must do is go back to the New Testament and discover how it happened at the beginning. If you read church history, you will find that all the great eras and epochs in the history of the Christian church, the times when she succeeded most of all and when masses of people were converted and added to the church, were always those periods when the church went back to the apostolic method. Indeed, I do not hesitate to make the assertion that you can try anything else you like, you can have your conferences and congresses and spend your millions in advertising, but it will achieve nothing finally. We must return to the apostolic method, and here the great apostle tells us exactly what he did and how it happened in this first age. There is no need to consider anything else whatsoever.

So, then, what did happen? The apostle tells us quite simply. Let me remind you of his position when he went to Thessalonica. Here is a little man, nothing much to look at. The Corinthians said, "His bodily presence is weak, and his speech contemptible" (2 Cor. 10:10). Paul did not look like a film star; he was most unprepossessing. He had just a few people with him when he went to this city. It was a pagan city, a part of Macedonia, what is now Greece. Its citizens had no biblical background. We are told today that the modern man cannot follow our preaching because he does not understand biblical terms such as *justification*. That is why some new translations or paraphrases of the Bible are brought out, and people feel that if only we had the Bible in everyday language, everybody would believe the message. Well, they did not understand the terms in Thessalonica either. They had no background whatsoever, as I shall show you. But the apostle went there, and as a result of his visit and his preaching, a church came into being.

And the apostle Paul tells us here exactly how it happened. It is an amazing summary of the apostolic method of evangelism. He tells us that there were two major factors. The first was the preaching of the apostles. This was essential. Our Lord had given the message to these men. He had given them the commission and the mandate. And they had gone out, and they had preached. This is always an essential. You must have preachers. We must have preachers in our homelands. We must have preachers in other lands that can still be described as pagan. Now I am a believer in books and in reading, but there is no question about this—it is the spoken word that has always been honored supremely by the Holy Spirit—preachers, truth mediated through personalities. And as you think of the teeming masses in many countries today—nations in South America, Asia, the Far East, and other parts of the world—you see the crying need for preachers, for men and women who will go, as these apostles went, over their part of the world preaching the gospel, preaching this message. Preachers are needed as much today as they have ever been.

Oh, I know that at the present time many say that the day of preaching is finished. We must have what is called "dialogue"—which means discussion—but *dialogue* sounds so much better! They say we must sit down and talk to people. Others say that all we must do is spend our time reading modern literature and studying modern art and drama and then go and talk to people about these subjects. And others say we must go in for politics and discuss politics and social conditions. All these new ideas and new methods are being put before us and praised and advocated. But I am here to remind you that God's method has always been the preaching of the gospel, and there has never been a greater need for preachers than at this present time. Nothing can substitute for preaching.

But that is only the first factor. There is a second. I wonder if you have ever noticed it as you read this chapter. There was a second vital factor in the spread of the gospel in the ancient world. What was that? It was the life and the witness and the testimony of the members of the Christian church. Paul says:

> And ye became followers of us, and of the Lord, having received the word in much affliction, with joy of the Holy Ghost. So that ye were ensamples to all that believe in Macedonia and Achaia. For from you sounded out the word of the Lord not only in Macedonia and Achaia, but also in every place your faith to God-ward is spread abroad; so that we need not to speak any thing. For they themselves shew of us what

manner of entering in we had unto you, and how ye turned to God from idols to serve the living and true God. (1 Thess. 1:6–9)

This is a most vital matter. What the apostle is really saying is this: You know, you good people, you members of the church of Thessalonica, you are making my preaching much easier. What I am finding now is that wherever I go and begin to preach, people stop me and say, "Ah, you're the man who preached in Thessalonica. We've heard about you. We've heard the news of what happened as the result of your speaking and preaching there." News about the amazing things that had happened to these people in the city of Thessalonica had spread abroad. Everybody was talking about it, not only in Macedonia and Achaia, but everywhere. And Paul says in essence, "There is a sense in which we do not need to speak anything now, because they know about it. The news about you has opened the doors for us, and the task has been made much easier."

This is a most important matter. I have sometimes feared that we are rapidly getting to the stage in which there will only be two or three preachers—if even that many—in the world. And the rest of the world will be listening to them on tapes or on television or something else. Everybody will be sitting back and listening, as if that is the way to evangelize the world. It is not! You need preachers, but you also need the testimony and the witness of the members of the church. Whatever the preaching, if it is not verified and substantiated by the lives of the people in the Christian church, it will be of no avail. And this is what the apostle tells us happened in his day and generation.

Now I confess that it was not until 1961 that I fully realized the tremendous implications of what Paul says here. It was in that year that I had the privilege of visiting the land of Greece. And then I realized something of what this chapter is saying. Paul says that the news spread abroad "not only in Macedonia." Let me give you a bit of geography. Thessalonica is up at the northeastern tip of Greece, and the hinterland, the section of country behind it—it is a seaport—was known as Macedonia. So it is not a bit surprising that what had happened under the preaching of the apostle in the town of Thessalonica was being talked about in Macedonia. But Paul says, "Not only in Macedonia and *Achaia*."

Achaia was the part of Greece that we now know as the Peloponnesian Peninsula, the part of Greece that is south of the Corinthian Canal. I discovered this in 1961, and it amazed me and lit up this whole passage for me. I did a journey from Corinth to Thessalonica, and I found it a most arduous trip. We had to cross a portion of sea. Then we went in a car, and we had to cross three high mountain ranges. It was quite a difficult journey even in 1961 since it is quite a considerable distance over the most difficult terrain. And yet the apostle says that news of what had happened up there in Thessalonica had spread all the way down over these great mountain ranges, right down to Achaia. They had no television. They had no radio. They had no telephone. They had no newspapers. But this astounding gospel was being talked of and was being spread from mouth to mouth, so that when Paul even went to the southernmost tip, they were ready for him and were waiting to receive his message.

Now this is a most important matter at the present time. We need preachers and evangelists, but equally we need men and women in our churches who open the door for the preacher, who proclaim the message in their lives, who attract people to come and listen to the gospel because of the marvelous things that happen to those who believe this message. The book of Acts frequently makes the point that ordinary church members as well as the apostles and other preachers spread this gospel, and this has been a leading factor in all great revivals and reformations. You find the same thing in the time of the Protestant Reformation. Everybody knew when people had become Protestants. They became objects of conversation and comment. The same is true of the Puritans in England, the Covenanters in Scotland, and the early Methodists. Everybody saw what had happened to them and talked about this astonishing change that had happened in the lives of these people. So they made others, perhaps merely out of a spirit of curiosity, go along to listen to the preaching that had produced such a result.

So the preaching of the gospel and the witness of Christian people combine together to present this message. These were the two great factors in the first century. They are also the two absolutely essential factors in our own century. But there is a third vital factor. The apos-

SETTING OUR AFFECTIONS UPON GLORY

tle puts it like this: *"Our gospel* came . . ."* (v. 5). What is the message of the Christian church? Alas that one has to ask the question! But one must ask it because there are people in the world—one meets them constantly—who think that the message of the Christian church is nothing but a protest against the war in Vietnam. They think that is Christianity. That is what they hear on television and on radio. That is what they hear from the lips of so many popular preachers. They think that Christianity is a protest against that war and other wars, a protest against the bombs. It is always a negative protest, a political, social message. But, my dear friends, by definition that is not the gospel.

The Christian message is a *gospel*, and the word *gospel* means good news. And so you see at once that these other topics are not the Christian message. It is not good news to protest against a war. But the essential Christian message is the most thrilling good news that has ever come into the world. That is how these people in Thessalonica received it, and that is how others heard about it. They said to one another, "There's an amazing message, a wonderful proclamation of great good news, a gospel!" And if what you and I preach and represent does not give people the impression that it is the most wonderful and glorious good news they have ever heard, then we are failing completely, and we are unworthy of the name *Christian*. "Our gospel"! Oh, let us never forget this. Let us be certain of the message.

Then Paul goes on to say this interesting thing: "Our gospel came not unto you *in word only*, but also . . ." When the apostle says that the gospel did not come "in word only," he means that it did come in word but not only in word. Is this clear to us, I wonder? Let me give you an illustration. A man may come to me and say, "I hear that you had a cold last week. Did you run a temperature as well?" He is saying that it is possible to have a cold without running a temperature but that you may have a cold with a temperature. So when Paul says, "Our gospel came not unto you in word only," he means that it did come in word, but there was something in addition to the word.

Why do I take the trouble to emphasize this point? Here again it is something that one is compelled to do, for the popular teaching today, the preaching that gets the publicity and the applause, is the preaching that tells us that the gospel does not come in word or in words. Christianity, it is said, is a wonderful spirit that possesses a person. A slogan a few years ago put it like this: "Christianity is caught, not taught." Yes, it is a marvelous spirit, a wonderful brotherhood with friendship, goodwill, and love to one another, a sort of "Christmas spirit." And people say, "This is Christianity. The great trouble in the past has been that too many theologians have said, 'It's this and it isn't that' and have described it and defined it in words and insisted upon particular doctrines. But this is entirely wrong." These people say, "Christianity is a quality of life—not so much a doctrine as a way of living." Well, that view is a complete and utter denial of what the great apostle tells us here and everywhere else and of what, indeed, the whole Bible tells us. The gospel comes in *word*, in *words*. And if it does not, it is not a true gospel.

But what are these words in which the gospel must always come? In a most extraordinary manner, the apostle gives us a summary in the last two verses of this one little chapter. "For they themselves shew of us what manner of entering in we had unto you, and how ye turned to God from idols to serve the living and true God; and to wait for his Son from heaven, whom he raised from the dead, even Jesus, which delivered us from the wrath to come." There are the words; so let us go in our imagination to listen to the apostle Paul preaching to these people in Thessalonica.

They were, pagans, not Jews. They had not been brought up with the Old Testament. They were polytheists, idolaters, and so on, living depraved lives, as we shall see. How did the apostle preach? What did he say to them? Here is the problem of communication, the problem of evangelism. These people were utterly without any knowledge of the terminology and of everything the apostle had to tell them. So what did he preach about? What is the Christian message? What are the words in which to convey it?

Paul started by telling the people about God. He writes in his epistle that they "turned to God from idols to serve the living and true God." He said to them in effect, "You good people, you are worshiping your idols, and you don't realize that you are doing something that's foolish and utterly vain. What are your idols? They're simply creatures that you've made yourselves." In those days, as you know, they would carve gods out of wood or make them of stone or some precious metal. Then they would say, "You are my god." And they would build a temple to their god. And then they would take their offerings and bow down and worship their god or gods. So Paul showed them the utter emptiness of this, that these gods were nothing but the projections of their own minds and imaginations, that they had no being, that they could not do anything. The people were just deluding and fooling themselves. This was idolatry!

We find this teaching also in the book of Acts. We find it in the Old Testament as well. The psalms deal with it in a very wonderful manner, full of divine sarcasm. Look at your gods, says the psalmist:

> They have mouths, but they speak not: eyes have they, but they see not: they have ears, but they hear not: noses have they, but they smell not: they have hands, but they handle not: feet have they, but they walk not: neither speak they through their throat. They that make them are like unto them. (Ps. 115:5–8)

Idolatry! The apostle started with that. That was the kind of life led by the citizens of Thessalonica, and Paul showed them the utter emptiness and vacuity of it all. But he did not stop merely at denunciation. He pointed out the seriousness of all this. He said in essence, "What makes it serious is that while you have been worshipping the gods that you have made yourselves, you have not been worshipping the only true and living God. You have been worshipping lies. There is nothing there. You called lies truth, but they are lies. There is a true God. You have worshipped dumb idols, useless objects, but there is a living God."

So the apostle began to tell these people about the God who had revealed himself to the children of Israel, the Jews. The God who had given a marvelous manifestation of himself in the Old Testament Scriptures is the true God. He is not a lie or a fabrication or the creation of the human mind. He is God from eternity to eternity, the author of all things, truth in himself, just and righteous and holy, the God who is "light, and in [whom] is no darkness at all" (1 John 1:5). Yes, but he is also the living God. And so the apostle told them about how this God had created the world out of nothing. He told them about the first verse in the Bible: "In the beginning God created the heaven and the earth." The living God. The God who interferes in the lives of people. The God of history. The God of providence. Paul gave them an exposition of the great message of the Old Testament and said in effect, "You have been ignorant of this. That is why you have made your dumb idols and have worshipped them. But here is the truth: you have all been made by God. And that is why this is so serious. That is why it is vital to you. If you die as you are, in your ignorance, worshipping your idols, you will go to condemnation, to everlasting misery."

The apostle talked about "the wrath to come" (v. 10). In other words, he told the people of Thessalonica that the God who had made the world had made man in his own image. He had given man certain powers and propensities. He had made him responsible. Paul told them that whether or not man realizes it, he has to give an account of himself to God—that "it is appointed unto men once to die, but after this the judgment" (Heb. 9:27). And he told these people that this great God, the only true and living God, is going to judge the whole world, including them, and that they would be judged according to the law that he had given to his people—the Ten Commandments and the moral law. These are the standards by which they were going to be judged. And Paul told them of the wrath to come and the eternal destiny that was to follow this judgment. He preached the true and the living God and showed them that all this was vital to their present position and to their eternal destiny. That was how the apostle preached.

It is only when you and I return to such preaching that we will be truly able to engage the interest and the attention of modern men and women, for the world is full of idolatry. It does not always take the same form. We are not as crude as they were in Thessalonica. People no longer make their idols in that way. They make them into other shapes—the shape, for instance, of automobiles—and they worship them. Literally! I know many men whose gods are their cars. They are always talking about them. They spend most of their time cleaning them, getting them to look better than somebody else's, often purchasing better models. They live for their cars. Others live for their houses. And I have known parents who literally worshipped their children. They thought about them, they schemed for them, they dreamed about them, they would sacrifice anything for their children. Their children were their gods. I have known wives who regarded their husbands as gods and husbands who regarded their wives as gods. They turned them into idols. The world is full of idolatry. Wealth. Sex. Prosperity. These are the things for which people are living. They are thrilled by them. They are moved by them. Their whole lives are governed by them. That is their religion. Those are their gods. The world is as full of idolatry today as it was in the first century. So what is needed is apostolic preaching that starts with the only true and living God, the one who is above all, the Judge of the ends of the earth and who tells us that everyone will have to stand before him.

"Well, dear me," says someone, "I thought you took a little time just now to say that the message of the church is what you call 'gospel,' good news. It doesn't sound very much like good news to me. You're preaching wrath and judgment and terror. Is that good news?"

Of course not. But it is the introduction to the good news. And I have a feeling that the masses are outside the Christian church today because we inside it have forgotten the introduction. Let me solemnly remind you of this: the gospel of Jesus Christ does not start even with the love of Jesus Christ. It starts with God. It is no use going to people and saying, "Come to Jesus" or "Come to Christ." They say, "We couldn't care less." Why? Because they have never seen any need of him. That is why they do not come to Christ. The only people who truly come to Christ are those who have seen their own condition under the condemnation of the law of God and know that one day they will face God in the eternal judgment, hearing the thunderings of Sinai. Knowing they will be confronted by the test, they realize they are utter and complete failures. Only such people are ready to listen to the gospel message concerning Jesus Christ and to fly to him as the only hope of salvation. The preaching of the message of the Christian church is a message that starts with God, the only true and living God. I say again that it is only as we realize our condition before God that we are ready to receive and to accept the message of the gospel.

What is the message of the gospel? We are familiar with it. This is where the church today starts, is it not, instead of starting with what the Puritans used to call a good "law work"? The trouble in the church today is that the law work has been neglected. There are too many people who have never repented. They do not know what repentance is. They have taken on Christ as a friend. They want to walk down the streets of life with heads erect. No, no! You must start with a law work. The law leads to the gospel, and there are no true conversions without a law work. You can bring people to religion, but that is very different from making Christians of them. But after they have heard the law, after they have seen their position, then comes the glorious gospel.

What, then, is the gospel? Here it is, in verse 10 of chapter 1: "And to wait for his Son from heaven, whom he raised from the dead, even Jesus." Having shown the people their terrible plight and predicament, the apostle began to tell them about Jesus. He told them about this man who had lived in Palestine. He told them about his extraordinary birth and then those quiet years when he just worked as a carpenter and how, at the age of thirty, he began to preach and the astonishing things that he did: his preaching, his understanding, and his miracles—Jesus. But who is Jesus? That is the question. People say, "The gospel doesn't come in words; you mustn't be theological; you don't need doctrine." But you cannot preach without it! The question is, who is Jesus? Was he only a man? If he was, we are all damned and hopeless. So who is Jesus? The apostle tells us here—"his Son from heaven." This is the doctrine of the incarnation. I say again that you cannot preach the gospel without doctrine. The very beginning of the gospel is to say, "When the fulness of the time was come, God sent forth his Son, made of a woman, made under the law, to redeem them that were under the law" (Gal. 4:4–5). Jesus Christ, Son of God, God and man, two natures in one person, unmixed, the person of Christ the Lord, attested by his miracles. Paul preached Jesus to them and told them who he was, that God had "visited and redeemed his people" (Luke 1:68). Jesus!

But then Paul went on to say that this Jesus "delivered us from the wrath to come." This is more theology, I am afraid. You cannot get away from doctrine. If you do not know the truth about the Lord, you are not a Christian, my friend. But what is this statement about his having "delivered" us? It means that Jesus did not come into the world just to teach us how to save ourselves. He did not come merely to give us an example. Jesus came in order to "deliver" us, and he has done the one thing that is essential to bring about that deliverance. What is that? Oh, this was the great theme of the apostle: "He hath made him to be sin for us, who knew no sin; that we might be made the righteousness of God in him" (2 Cor. 5:21). "God was in Christ, reconciling the world unto himself, not imputing their trespasses unto them" (2 Cor. 5:19). God has taken our trespasses and imputed them to Christ, laid them upon him, made him to be sin, smote him, struck him: "We did esteem him stricken, smitten of God" (Isa. 53:4). This is the great doctrine of the atonement. You cannot be a Christian without this. You can be a pacifist, a Socialist, and many other things, but you cannot be a Christian. This is the essence of Christianity—that the Son of God came into the world in order to take our sins in his own body on the tree, in order to receive our punishment: "by whose stripes ye were healed" (1 Pet. 2:24). This is what Paul preached to the Thessalonians. The theology of the atonement, the doctrine of the atonement, the substitution, the fulfillment of what John the Baptist said: "Behold the Lamb of God, which taketh away the sin of the world" (John 1:29). Christ dying on the cross, the innocent dying for the guilty, the good dying for the evil: "Who his own self bare our sins in his own body on the tree" (1 Pet. 2:24). And he died, and they laid him in a tomb.

Is that the end? No, no! "And to wait for his Son from heaven, whom he raised from the dead" (1 Thess. 1:10). What is this? It is the doctrine of the resurrection. There is no gospel apart from the literal, physical resurrection of Jesus Christ. Let the clever scholars say what they will. Let them attempt to philosophize it away, as some were trying to do in Corinth so long ago. It all comes to nothing. We are saved by the fact that Christ literally rose from the dead, having accomplished the grand atonement. "If Christ be not risen, then is our preaching vain, and your faith is also vain" (1 Cor. 15:14). You are then still in your sins, and you are under condemnation. "[Christ] was delivered for our offences," says Paul to the Romans, "and was raised again for our justification" (Rom. 4:25). The resurrection is God's proclamation to the whole cosmos that the Son's work is complete, that he finished it, that the law is satisfied, God is satisfied. The resurrection, the literal, physical resurrection, also gave the final proof that Jesus of Nazareth was indeed the Son of God: "declared to be the Son of God with power, according to the spirit of holiness, by the resurrection from the dead" (Rom. 1:4). Here it is, the doctrine of the resurrection.

But Paul still was not finished! ". . . and to wait for his Son from heaven." He not only rose from the dead, he ascended. Do you remember the ascension? The Lord Jesus Christ ascended, passed through the heavens, and took his seat at the right hand of God. And there he is, seated, "expecting till his enemies be made his footstool" (Heb. 10:13). But this is not the end. There is a day when he will come again: "to wait for his Son from heaven." The Son of God will come back into the world, and he will come not for salvation this time but for judgment. He will not come as the babe of Bethlehem. He will come as the King of kings and the Lord of lords riding the clouds of heaven, and he will come to "judge the [whole] world in righteousness" (Acts 17:31). He will destroy sin and evil and all that belong to that realm and will set up his glorious kingdom of righteousness and peace.

> Jesus shall reign where'er the sun
> Doth his successive journeys run;
> His kingdom stretch from shore to shore,
> Till moons shall wax and wane no more.
>
> ISAAC WATTS

The whole universe will be restored to its pristine condition and, perhaps even more, will be glorified, and the Son will hand back the perfect kingdom to the Father, and God shall be all and in all. That was what Paul preached in Thessalonica. And you cannot do that in twenty minutes, can you? Christian people, if you object to the preaching of the gospel, you are denying the gospel. This is the message, and you must not leave out any part of it. The gospel comes in word, in words, and those were the words then, and they are still the words now.

But if I were to stop at that point, in a sense my preaching would be in vain. That alone does not account for the spread of the gospel and the rising of Christian churches in the first century or in any other century. The apostle writes, "Our gospel came not unto you in word only, but also in power, and in the Holy Ghost, and in much assurance" (v. 5). Here is the whole secret not only of the apostle Paul but of all the great, true evangelists throughout the centuries. Here is the secret of the Protestant fathers, those Puritan preachers, Whitefield and the others in the eighteenth century. What does Paul mean by saying, "but also in power, and in the Holy Ghost, and in much assurance"? To whom does the assurance apply?

In the first instance, the assurance applied to the apostle himself. "Do you know," says Paul in effect, "when I was preaching to you at Thessalonica, I was not simply uttering words, but I knew I was clothed with the Holy Spirit. I knew that I was nothing but a little channel and a vehicle and that the Almighty God, the Holy Spirit, was using me and was driving my words to your minds and hearts and consciences. I did it with assurance. I knew!"

The position seemed hopeless. What was there for Paul to build on when preaching to these people who were so ignorant? They knew nothing. They had been living lives of debauchery and evil and sin and vileness. He describes this in so many places—in the second half of the first chapter of Romans, in 1 Corinthians 6, and so on. That is how they were living in this seaport town of Thessalonica. What did Paul have to go on? The Holy Spirit. He felt the power, and he had great assurance that he was being used. The apostle was so concerned about this that he described it in a little more detail in the next chapter.

> As we were allowed of God to be put in trust with the gospel, even so we speak; not as pleasing men, but God, which trieth our hearts. For neither at any time used we flattering words, as ye know, nor a cloke of covetousness; God is witness: nor of men sought we glory, neither of

you, nor yet of others, when we might have been burdensome, as the apostles of Christ. (1 Thess. 2:4–6)

Do you realize what the apostle Paul is saying? He never sought to please people. You cannot imagine the apostle Paul tripping lightly onto a platform and then cracking a few jokes just to put the audience right. The thing is unthinkable! It is insulting to the very name of the great apostle. He had no tricks. He had no methods, no manipulation of lights and music and other things in order to get people into the right condition to receive his message. No, no! He eschewed it all. "I determined not to know any thing among you, save Jesus Christ, and him crucified" (1 Cor. 2:2). "And my speech and my preaching was not with enticing words of man's wisdom" (1 Cor. 2:4). He knew all about Greek rhetoric and all the tricks of oratory. He dismissed them. He rejected them. He hated them. And here he repeats it again. He never used flattering words, never ingratiated himself with the audience. No, no! He was a herald of the gospel. He proclaimed the words of the message, and the Spirit was upon him. His total reliance was on the Spirit of the living God. He had assurance of it: "in power, and in the Holy Ghost, and in much assurance" (1 Thess. 1:5). That has been the characteristic of the church and her preachers in every period of reformation and of revival, and there is no hope for us until we return to this. We must be fools for Christ's sake and be willing to be laughed at and derided by the world as we trust to the message and the power of the Holy Spirit upon it.

But Paul says that the Holy Spirit was also working in the Christians in Thessalonica. And he must have been, for how could ignorant pagan people with no background have any connection with such a message? It was the Holy Spirit's work. At first as they listened to the apostle, they did not know what he was talking about, but gradually they began to feel that he was speaking to them and that this was true. Something was gripping them. Something was moving them. One after another they said, "It's right. It's true of me." And they were troubled and unhappy about themselves. They had never heard this before, but it became living and real. They were convinced and convicted. And they saw their terrible predicament. Then they heard this wonderful message of the gospel, and they believed it and they submitted to it. Paul says, "And ye became followers of us, and of the Lord, having received the word in much affliction, with joy of the Holy Ghost" (v. 6).

But these Christian people also gave proof that they had really received the word of salvation and truly believed it. What was the evidence? In verse 9 Paul writes: "They themselves shew of us what manner of entering in we had unto you, and how ye turned to God from idols to serve the living and true God." This is the test of whether or not we have received the message. Not that we come forward at the end of a meeting or sign a card and then wonder next day what we have done and in a few weeks find ourselves back where we were before. No, no! The evidence is this—that you leave your idols. You turn your back on them. You turn from idols to the living and the true God, and you begin to serve him, which means that you begin to worship him. He becomes the Lord of your life, and you live to his glory and to his praise. You now put into practice the answer to the first question of the Shorter Catechism of the Westminster Confession: "What is the chief end of man? Man's chief end is to glorify God and to enjoy him for ever. . . . serve the living and true God."

And the Thessalonians gave further evidence: "Ye became followers of us"—they listened to the apostles, and they joined their company—"and of the Lord"—they became members of the Christian church (v. 6). And notice that this was not a kind of flash in the pan, nor was it just easy believism. "Remembering," Paul says in verse 3, "without ceasing your work of faith"—"Faith, if it hath not works, is dead" (James 2:17)—"and labour of love, and patience of hope." They did not stop; they went on and persisted and gave themselves to it. It became the biggest thing in their lives. This was their great characteristic. And, still more amazing, they "received the word in much affliction"—persecution, derision, sarcasm, and scorn, but it made no difference to them—"with joy of the Holy Ghost" (v. 6). You could do what you liked to these early Christians, but you would never make them deny the faith. You could ostracize them, it did not matter. You could put them to death, throw them to the lions in the arena, it made no difference. They persevered in spite of the affliction, in the affliction, "with joy of the Holy Ghost." They did not give up. The result was, as Paul tells them, that they had become a phenomenon, and everybody was talking about them. Everybody in Thessalonica was talking about them. Everybody all the way through Macedonia and over the mountain ranges and down in Achaia, everybody everywhere in the then-known civilized world was talking about this phenomenon. And this is the only hope for us at this present time.

Come with me for a final visit to Thessalonica. Do you see that group of people standing there on the street corner? They are talking together about politics, the injustice of the Roman Empire, the imposition of taxes upon them, and so on, exactly as people do now. Then a man suddenly passes by, and one of the group says to another, "Do you recognize him?"

The other man looks and says, "No, I don't know him."

"Of course you do, that's so-and-so."

"Impossible!" They had always known the man as a drunkard, an adulterer, a wife beater, one of the worst men in Thessalonica. But here he is, entirely changed. His very appearance is different. His face is different. Everything about him is different. So the second man then asks, "What on earth has happened to him?"

"Well, you know," says the first man, "he's been like this ever since a man called Paul came here. You remember what he used to be like. But, you know, this strange little preacher came here with this extraordinary message, and when this man who used to be a drunkard heard it, he became absolutely different, and he's been different ever since. He's going now to what they call a prayer meeting, and he seems to be going constantly. He's a new man. His wife is different too. His children are different. His home is different. I've never seen such a change in a man in my whole life. It's amazing. It's extraordinary."

By now the curiosity of the second man is aroused.

Then a woman goes past, and the first man asks, "Do you recognize her?"

"I've no idea who she is."

"Dear me," says the first man, "that's so-and-so." And he mentions one of the worst women in the city, an adulteress, a woman who was never at home and who neglected her husband. Her children were in rags. She did not prepare the right food for them and neglected their health. She was a woman hardly worthy of the name of woman. But there she goes now, neatly dressed. And she is going to this same meeting, a prayer meeting or a preaching meeting. And, again, her home is changed, her children are different, her husband is different.

This is what was happening under the preaching of this gospel, which had come "in demonstration of the Spirit and of power" (1 Cor. 2:4). These people had been born again. They were renewed. They were entirely changed. They were saints adorning the church of God.

Here is my question for you: Are you a phenomenon in the city where you live? Are you an object of wonder to your neighbors and associates? It is only when you and I, who are members of the church, are people like this and become phenomena, objects of conversation and of curiosity, that we shall begin to see revival and renewal in the church. Oh yes, the preaching, the Word, the only gospel, and the power of the Spirit upon it are all essential. But the proof of its truth is in the daily lives of the members of the church, people who claim to be Christians and who belong to the only true and living God. My dear friends, let us make certain of the message, but let us pray without ceasing that God shall send down his mighty Spirit of power upon us who have the privilege of preaching and upon all who listen. Let us pray for true spiritual awakening and revival, and let us do so until God in his infinite kindness and condescension shall be pleased to hear us and to open the windows of heaven again and send down such a shower of blessing that we shall scarcely be able to contain it. That is how Christianity spread in the first century. That is how it spread in every other century, and it is the only way in which it will spread in this century.

O Lord, our God, have mercy upon us. Forgive us especially, we pray again, for our folly, for foolish talking about our century and the modern man, as if anything has changed. Awaken us, we pray, and bring us to see that your method is still the same, that the truth remains unchanged and unchanging, and that the power of the blessed Holy Spirit is in no sense diminished. Lord, hear us. "Revive thy work, O Lord, thy mighty arm make bare. Speak with the voice that wakes the dead, and make thy people hear." And unto you and unto you alone shall we give all the praise and the honor and the glory both now and forever. Amen.

7

THE HIGHWAY
TO REVIVAL

☼

And the LORD said unto Moses, Depart, and go up hence, thou and the people which thou hast brought up out of the land of Egypt.

EXODUS 33:1

I should like us now to consider the message of chapter 33 of the book of Exodus, and I want to call your attention to the entire chapter because this is a bit of history. It is an incident in the life of Moses and the children of Israel, and I do not want so much to concentrate on any particular statement as upon the total action that Moses took on this occasion.

Now the events described in chapter 33 took place after the children of Israel had passed through a most serious crisis, one of the worst they had faced. God had called Moses up onto the mount that he might give him the law, the commandments, and Moses had been there with God for forty days. The children of Israel, left down below in the plain under the care of Aaron, had, after a while, become restive and had said in effect, "Where is this Moses? We don't know what's happened to him. Let's forget all about him." And they had asked Aaron to make a god. At his suggestion they had given him all the gold they had, and all this was melted down and was made into a golden calf. Then the people had begun to worship this golden calf. But not only that—they had started drinking and dancing and engaging in sin and in open immorality.

Then we have a tremendous picture of Moses coming down the mountain and hearing all this and being amazed and alarmed and scarcely knowing what to do. But taking the situation in hand, he turned to the people and said, "Ye have sinned a great sin: and now I will go up unto the LORD; peradventure I shall make an atonement for your sin" (Ex. 32:30). Then this is what we read:

> And Moses returned unto the LORD, and said, Oh, this people have sinned a great sin, and have made them gods of gold. Yet now, if thou wilt forgive their sin—; and if not, blot me, I pray thee, out of thy book which thou hast written. And the LORD said unto Moses, Whosoever hath sinned against me, him will I blot out of my book. Therefore now go, lead the people unto the place of which I have spoken unto thee: behold, mine Angel shall go before thee: nevertheless in the day when I visit I will visit their sin upon them. And the LORD plagued the people, because they made the calf, which Aaron made. (Ex. 32:31–35)

And then we come to the thirty-third chapter, with the history that it records. Now it seems to me that in chapter 32 we have the church in a state of terrible declension, a backslidden church, a church that has rebelled against God and gone its own way. And in chapter 33 we are given the account of how Moses reacted to that condition, what he did about it in order to restore the church. That is why I am calling attention to this chapter. I feel that it has a very contemporary message to give us; it presents us with far too accurate a picture of and parallel to what obtains among us at this present time. In other words, here, it seems to me, we are given an account and a description of what I would call the highway to revival.

Now when I talk about revival, I do not mean an organized evangelistic campaign. That is not revival. A revival is a visitation of the Spirit of God, a mighty movement within the whole body of the church. Revival applies and pertains to the church herself rather than to the outsider. The outsider only derives the benefits from it. A revival is a revivification, a re-enlivening of the church herself. That is the true definition of revival, and it is because we have in this chapter an account of the essential steps to revival that I am calling your attention to it. I suggest to you that in this history we are presented very clearly with four stages or steps to revival, and all I want to do is to show you these four steps as they are outlined to us here.

The first step starts at verse 30 in chapter 32 and goes to the end of verse 6 of chapter 33. What is it? It is when those who are spiritual, alive and alert, identify with the problem of the people. Moses has not been guilty of any sin at all. But he identifies himself with the condition of the people, and he intercedes on their behalf in that astonishing prayer. See this pause, this gap, this dash, as it were: "If thou wilt forgive their sin—; and if not, blot me, I pray thee, out of thy book" (v. 32). Moses' words are reminiscent of the apostle Paul's words with regard to his fellow countrymen, the Jews, when they were rejecting the gospel: "I could wish that myself were accursed from Christ for my brethren, my kinsmen according to the flesh," that is, his fellow Jews (Rom. 9:3).

Now the principle here is that the problem becomes our burden. We do not talk about "them," as it were, but we identify ourselves with them. We are a part of the condition they are in. We become concerned. Furthermore, we must realize, if we have spiritual understanding, that we have a certain responsibility in the matter. The mass of the people here at the foot of the mountain are ignorant. They did not realize what they were doing. But Moses does. So he takes the burden and the leadership upon himself. And this is something, again, that you will always find in the history of all the great revivals that have taken place in the story of the Christian church. It may be just one man who feels the burden, who does not merely bemoan the conditions but becomes burdened about it, feels a personal responsibility, and knows that he must do something. And that is what Moses does here. He delivers the message of God to the people without fear, in a very courageous manner (Ex. 33:5). He speaks to them, calls them to repent, and shows them the truth about what they have been doing.

Now this is never a pleasant thing to have to do. Indeed, it is always very painful. But it is characteristic of Moses, as it has always been of those whom God has used to deal with his church. Look at poor Jeremiah. He did not want to say the things that he said. More than once he decided not to, but he could not help it. The word of God was like a fire in his bones, and he had to speak. It becomes the duty of any who really understand the times in which we are living to speak plainly and clearly. If you want popularity, of course, you will not do this. But if you want to serve God, you will have to speak the truth and denounce sin and error in the church without fear or favor. And so you become a kind of intercessor. You stand between the masses of the people, who seem to be so ignorant, and the living God, and you mediate between them. You take their confession to God, and you take his message to them, and you do this with the extraordinary boldness that Moses manifests on this occasion.

Now consider the second step:

> And Moses took the tabernacle, and pitched it without the camp, afar off from the camp, and called it the Tabernacle of the congregation. And it came to pass, that every one which sought the LORD went out unto the tabernacle of the congregation, which was without the camp. And it came to pass, when Moses went out unto the tabernacle, that all the people rose up, and stood every man at his tent door, and looked after Moses, until he was gone into the tabernacle. And it came to pass, as Moses entered into the tabernacle, the cloudy pillar descended, and stood at the door of the tabernacle, and the LORD talked with Moses. And all the people saw the cloudy pillar stand at the tabernacle door: and all the people rose up and worshipped, every man in his tent door. And the LORD spake unto Moses face to face, as a man speaketh unto his friend. And he turned again into the camp: but his servant Joshua, the son of Nun, a young man, departed not out of the tabernacle. (Ex. 33:7–11)

Now here is a very significant move, and perhaps the most controversial move that Moses takes. But I do want to emphasize it, because I want to show that this has been an inevitable step, always, in the long story of the revival of the Christian church. Notice what Moses does. We are told that he "took the tabernacle, and pitched it without the camp, afar off from the camp, and called it the Tabernacle of the congregation."

Let us be clear about this. This is not the tabernacle that was built later according to God's instructions, in which the people presented their burnt offerings and sacrifices. This is a tabernacle of meeting, and the striking thing we are told is that until this point in the journey of the children of Israel, this tent, this tabernacle, has been in the midst of the camp. But in view of what had happened, Moses makes this drastic decision. He takes this tabernacle and removes it far off, outside the camp. Why does he do this? Well, it seems to me to be perfectly clear. It is in order that the people might have peace and quiet to worship God and to meditate truly. He does not do this merely for the sake of having some special spiritual enjoyment for himself and for those who happen to agree with him. It is not the kind of separation that the Pharisees, in their self-righteousness, were guilty of. It is a desire for quiet, for peace, out of the hubbub and the noise and the bustle and the business of the life of the camp, amid the totality of the people. It is a drawing aside in order that, with greater intensity and greater purity, the people might worship God and discover what he would have them do.

Now here is a most important principle, and it is interesting to trace it in the history of the church over the running centuries. This has generally been the first real move in the direction of a purified, revived church. There is a sense, of course, in which this is what happened in the New Testament itself. Although our Lord and others continued to attend synagogue worship, there was also this drawing apart, and as you go on reading the New Testament, you see this element coming out more and more strongly until eventually the Christian church was entirely separate from the Jewish religion and synagogue worship. But at first there was the kind of situation that you find here—a group of people who see the truth together and draw themselves aside. They go out of the camp, as it were, in order that they might meet with God in this intimate and more real manner.

Let me jump across the centuries. Take what happened in several countries even before the Protestant Reformation. You have, for example, the Waldensian gathering of people in northern Italy. They still, in a sense, belonged to the Roman Catholic Church, but they had been awakened. They had been quickened. They had seen the state of the Roman Catholic Church. They had seen what a travesty it was of the true church and the true gospel. So they would draw apart and meet in caves on the mountains. They would meet in secret to study the Word and to pray. In Bohemia and Moravia and parts of Holland similar movements were formed by Christians who were known as the Brethren of the Common

Life, and their leaders included the great John Hus. All these groups did exactly what Moses did.

Moses takes this tabernacle outside the camp not only so that he himself might go there and worship, but the people too. "It came to pass, that every one which sought the LORD went out unto the tabernacle of the congregation, which was without the camp" (v. 7). The bulk of the people do not go. We are told, "All the people rose up, and stood every man at his tent door, and looked after Moses, until he was gone into the tabernacle" (v. 8). They are bewildered by Moses' strange action. They do not know what he is doing, and probably they are highly critical of him. The children of Israel were frequently critical of Moses, their great leader, because they did not have spiritual insight and understanding. A man like Moses is inevitably going to be misunderstood. It does not matter. They just stand there and look on in amazement, but Moses knows what he is doing. And there are others who know, and they join him and go out to the tabernacle.

Not only did that happen frequently before the Protestant Reformation, but it happened even afterward. Many of the churches that had become Protestant and in a very general sense "reformed" were not satisfactory to many Christian people. In England, for instance, we had the great Puritan movement. The Puritans were a group of people who simply did what Moses does here. They drew themselves aside. They belonged to the body, but they realized that this was not sufficient. They knew they must meet together and worship God and encourage one another and discover a better way. They wanted a more purified type of worship. And again they were misunderstood and were derided. The very term *Puritan* is a term of derision. But these people really were anxious to seek the Lord and to serve him truly.

A similar situation in Scotland was that of the Covenanters. But perhaps the Pilgrim Fathers are the greatest illustration. These people left England because they were not allowed to worship in the way they deemed to be true. They escaped first to Holland, and then they wanted to come to a new land where they could worship God in a scriptural manner. They separated themselves. They drew apart. Eventually they came to North America and played a major role in the founding of the great country of the USA. That is but a repetition of what Moses does in Exodus 33. The Pilgrim Fathers did not come to America to make money. They came to worship God in a pure manner and to get his blessing. They felt it was impossible in the church as she then was in England, and that was why they came.

Indeed, this went on even in the following century, the eighteenth century. When the church, again, was in a sinful, mixed, unhappy state, the Evangelical Awakening came—Methodism in its various branches, Calvinistic Methodism under Whitefield, another type of Methodism under the Wesley brothers. All those who were quickened and alive spiritually realized they were not getting any food or help in the church, so they drew together. They formed little societies, little associations. At first it was informal. Then they gradually organized themselves, and there were more and more of these units or cells. Everybody who became spiritually awakened joined one of these groups, and there they spent their time together; they were filled with the Spirit, and they were enabled to preach, and a great revival took place.

So this is a very important principle. But let me return to the Methodist awakening. Its very early beginnings are most interesting. A number of young men were students at the University of Oxford. All of them were young. The oldest was John Wesley himself, who was in his mid-twenties. Charles Wesley, John Wesley's younger brother, was dissatisfied with the religious life of England, and of Oxford in particular. He and others were there to be trained for the ministry, but they felt that the life that was being lived was a sinful life, a travesty of Christianity. And Charles became so concerned that he suggested that a number of them who felt the same should meet together to study, to read the New Testament in Greek, to pray to God, and to see what good they could do by visiting prisoners and relieving the sufferings of the poor. So they would meet together, generally once a week. And they became known as "the Holy Club." Again this was a term of criticism— "the Holy Club," "the Methodists," these people who believed in living in a methodical and spiritual manner. They started as just a small company, but out of that the great Evangelical Awakening took place. When Whitefield went up as a young student to Oxford, he heard of this "Holy Club," and he jumped at the opportunity of belonging to it, and there he received the mighty influence that made him the first great leader in the Evangelical Awakening.

So this is our principle. You find it in the Scriptures and ever since in the history of the church. Those who feel the burden of the times, those who grieve for the state of the church, do not just talk about it, they do something further. They get together. It must be done. They meet in peace and quiet where they can confer together and pray together and study the Scriptures together and discover the will of the Lord together. It is this movement of taking the tabernacle out of the camp, far away from the camp, because the majority do not understand. This is regrettable, but it is open to anyone who wants to go there, to go out from the camp. "And it came to pass, that every one which sought the LORD went out unto the tabernacle of the congregation" (v. 7).

And here we find Moses going out repeatedly and there meeting with the Lord, and then we read, "And the LORD spake unto Moses face to face, as a man speaketh unto his friend" (v. 11). God clearly approves of Moses' action. He praises his servant. He gives him encouragement. Even the people in their ignorance feel that something is happening. "And all the people saw the cloudy pillar stand at the tabernacle door: and all the people rose up and worshipped, every man in his tent door" (v. 10). You must not wait for the mass of people before you take action. But when you see this happening, act upon it. Act together, and the people at last will begin to sense that something real and true is taking place, and numbers will follow, not quite knowing what they are doing. So there they stand and worship, "every man in his tent door." Here is a vital step, and God honors it. God puts his seal upon it. God blesses Moses in this way.

Just a final note before we leave this second stage. Notice the last statement in verse 11: "And he [Moses] turned again into the camp: but his servant Joshua, the son of Nun, a young man, departed not out of the tabernacle." This means that Moses who, after all, is the great leader of the people in every sense, has business to do in the camp. He would like to spend the whole of his time in the tabernacle, but he does not. He cannot. He has to do his work. So he has to keep going back to the camp. But he always leaves Joshua, the son of Nun, this young servant of his, permanently in the tabernacle. I think this is very wonderful. Joshua is left there just to wait for an answer that God might suddenly give. Moses is praying in faith. You never know when the answer is coming, so Joshua stays there. God might suddenly reveal something, might say something. Joshua is the representation of the expectancy, the faith, of the praying church, waiting for a word from God and always ready to receive it and to act upon it.

Now I have no doubt at all but that many of us, had we been in the position of Moses, would have been more than satisfied with all this. Take even that first stage. When Moses intercedes on behalf of the people, God says that he will send them up into the land. He says:

> Behold, mine Angel shall go before thee. . . . And the LORD said unto Moses, Depart, and go up hence, thou and the people which thou hast brought up out of the land of Egypt, unto the land which I sware unto Abraham, to Isaac, and to Jacob, saying, Unto thy seed will I give it: And I will send an angel before thee; and I will drive out the Canaanite, the Amorite, and the Hittite, and the Perizzite, the Hivite, and the Jebusite: unto a land flowing with milk and honey. (Ex. 32:34; 33:1–3)

I am afraid that most of us would have been more than satisfied even with that. Here is a promise of being led by an angel to the land flowing with milk and honey. But Moses will not accept it; it is not good enough for him. He does not want success. He does not merely want ease and comfort. He wants more. God offers an angel to lead them, but Moses will not accept it.

Then in this second stage you would have thought that when God, as it were, comes to meet him face-to-face, Moses would have been more than satisfied. I think most of us would have been, but Moses is not. There is a kind of divine impatience upon those who really have spiritual enlightenment and see the true state of the church and the only solution. Moses is dissatisfied. So we go on to stage three.

SETTING OUR AFFECTIONS UPON GLORY

And Moses said unto the LORD, See, thou sayest unto me, Bring up this people: and thou hast not let me know whom thou wilt send with me. Yet thou hast said, I know thee by name, and thou hast also found grace in my sight. Now therefore, I pray thee, if I have found grace in thy sight, shew me now thy way, that I may know thee, that I may find grace in thy sight: and consider that this nation is thy people. And he [God] said, My presence shall go with thee, and I will give thee rest. And he said unto him, If thy presence go not with me, carry us not up hence. For wherein shall it be known here that I and thy people have found grace in thy sight? is it not in that thou goest with us? so shall we be separated, I and thy people, from all the people that are upon the face of the earth. And the LORD said unto Moses, I will do this thing also that thou hast spoken: for thou hast found grace in my sight, and I know thee by name. (vv. 12–17)

Here now is another vital step. In a sense this is where real urgent prayer truly begins in this story. There had been prayer before, but now it becomes urgent. And there has never been a revival in the long history of the church except it has passed through this stage, this urgency in prayer. Moses, you see, shows that he is discontented still. He wants more. He wants something further. So he prays and pleads and intercedes with God. Let me just give you an analysis of his prayer so that you can work it out for yourselves in detail and at your leisure.

To start with, *what* does Moses pray for? First, he prays for a personal assurance: "that I may know thee" (v. 13). He is not asking to know *about* God. He already has that knowledge. He has already met with him on the mount. This word "know" is a very strong term. Moses wants an intimate, personal knowledge of God. That is what he is after. And it is only when we get to this stage that we really begin to function truly as Christians. A general belief in God and a knowledge about God and about salvation—the very least in the church has that. Here is a man who wants more. He is pressing on to a personal, direct, and intimate knowledge of God.

Second, Moses prays for power: "If thy presence go not with me, carry us not up hence" (v. 15). The task is great, and Moses knows he is inadequate. He cannot trust himself. He is the meekest of men. So as he realizes the magnitude of the problem and his own weakness, he prays to God for his presence and his power. My dear friends, we must not forget this. We must be orthodox, and we must fight for orthodoxy, but orthodoxy alone will not win the battle. We need the power of God as well as his truth. We need this special authentication of our position. That is what Moses is pleading for. That is why he refuses the leadership even of an angel. He will not take anything less than the very presence of God in living, real power in the midst of the people. That is what he prays for.

Next, *why* does Moses pray this prayer? It is because his ultimate concern is for the glory of God. That is what he is interested in. "For wherein shall it be known here that I and thy people have found grace in thy sight? is it not in that thou goest with us?" (v. 16). He is concerned about the name of God. They are God's people; they claim that, and everybody knows them as such. But here they are, in this miserable plight. They have been behaving in that disgraceful, idolatrous, sinful manner, and the nations will judge God by this. So Moses is concerned about the glory of God. And this should be our concern. If you are only concerned about your particular church or denomination, you do not belong to this realm at all. We are not simply to salvage denominations or save some particular tradition. We should be concerned about the glory of God and his great and holy name, for it is being spat upon in the church and in the world at this present time.

But then, having started with the glory of God, Moses is concerned about the honor of the church also: "For wherein shall it be known here that I and thy people have found grace in thy sight? . . . so shall we be separated, I and thy people, from all the people that are upon the face of the earth" (v. 16). Those people whom God has used throughout the centuries have had a great and glorious conception of the Christian church. She is not just a human institution. She is a spiritual society, a church of the firstborn. And it grieves their hearts to see her in rags and in worldliness and in utter confusion. Do we have this concern for the honor and the name of the Christian church? And do we long to see her functioning as a church, uttering no uncertain sound but the certain sound of the gospel and clothed with might and power and honor and glory?

Moses is concerned. He is jealous not only for the name of the Lord but also for the condition of God's people.

Also, of course, in the third place, and it follows inevitably, Moses is anxious that the heathen round and about them should know about God. "Now therefore, I pray thee, if I have found grace in thy sight, shew me now thy way, that I may know thee, that I may find grace in thy sight: and consider that this nation is thy people" (v. 13), and that all these nations that are round and about may know, in order that they may be humbled and subdued and in turn awakened and inquire in essence, "Who are these people, and how can we know their God?" That is why Moses prays for power.

And that brings me to the third point in this analysis of Moses' prayer—the *way* in which he prays, and this is truly astonishing. Do you notice his boldness and his confidence? Do you notice the element of reasoning? And yet at the same time do you see how orderly his prayer is, how specific, and, above all, how urgent?

Let me start with the boldness. Have you ever thought of this? Listen to Moses speaking to Almighty God: "And Moses said unto the LORD, See . . ." "See"! He is having an argument with God. And God, I believe, likes this. God is our Father. We are to do everything with reverence and godly fear. But we are the children of God, and there is a kind of holy boldness. Moses says, "See, thou sayest unto me, Bring up this people: and thou hast not let me know whom thou wilt send with me. Yet thou hast said, I know thee by name, and thou hast also found grace in my sight. Now therefore, I pray thee, if I have found grace in thy sight, shew me now thy way" (vv. 12–13). This is a child reasoning with his father, reminding the father of what he has already said, using it as an argument, entering into a kind of dispute, saying, "But you know you've said this, and yet why aren't you doing it?" This is true importunate prayer.

The old saints of the nineteenth century and, still more, of the eighteenth and the seventeenth centuries often used to pray as Moses does here. They would plead God's own promises to him. They knew their Scriptures, and their prayers were scriptural. They would take the promises of the Scriptures and hold them up before God and say, "This is what you said." And they would reason and say "if" and "therefore." Do we know anything about this kind of praying? It is not surprising that the church is as she is. We must learn how to pray, how to intercede, how to plead with God, how to draw, as some of the old saints used to put it, on the cords of the promises. The promises are a kind of rope that goes up to heaven, and you pull on the rope until you pull down the answer to the promises of God. He has let down the rope. Hold on to it and pull and keep on pulling until God has granted the blessing. That is how Moses prays. This boldness, this confidence, this reasoning, this orderliness—this is true intercession.

There has never been revival in the church except there has been a band of intercessors like this who have drawn themselves apart, taking the burden with them. Whatever may be the case with the masses of the people, they have not waited. They have acted, and they have pleaded with God. And again God obviously approves of this type of praying and encourages it because he says to Moses, "I will do this thing also that thou hast spoken: for thou hast found grace in my sight, and I know thee by name" (v. 17). This is a great mystery, of course. And if you begin to try to understand it theologically, you will go mad. How can a man persuade God? In a sense he cannot; in another sense he can. Let us never forget that the almighty, sovereign, eternal God is our Father. I believe he likes to hear his children arguing and pleading the promises, and he will say, "Yes, I will do this also for you." Moses, as it were, leads God on from step to step and stage to stage. This is just God's way of working, so that we are involved in it. And this is how we grow and develop.

Once more I do not think I am risking very much when I say that all of us would be more than satisfied if God said to us, "I will do this thing also that thou hast spoken" (v. 17). We would have stopped long ago, would we not? Milk and honey. Good times. A prosperous church. Wonderful! No, no! says Moses. He is not satisfied even now. So we go on to stage four.

> And he [Moses] said, I beseech thee, shew me thy glory. And he [God] said, I will make all my goodness pass before thee, and I will proclaim the name of the LORD before thee; and will be gracious to whom I will

be gracious, and will shew mercy on whom I will shew mercy. And he said, Thou canst not see my face: for there shall no man see me, and live. And the LORD said, Behold, there is a place by me, and thou shalt stand upon a rock: and it shall come to pass, while my glory passeth by, that I will put thee in a clift of the rock, and will cover thee with my hand while I pass by: and I will take away mine hand, and thou shalt see my back parts: but my face shall not be seen. (vv. 18–23)

That is revival. What does it mean? Well, having had a taste of these things, Moses is not satisfied. He wants more. He says, "I beseech thee, shew me thy glory." He wants really to see God, and the glory of God, with his naked eye. But here he goes too far, and God has to tell him that this cannot happen, that no one can see God with their physical eyes and live. Saul of Tarsus, on the road to Damascus, had just a glimpse of the glorified Christ, and it blinded him. But Moses makes his request, and God does not crush him. He says in effect, "You cannot see my face, but I will tell you what I will do for you. I will give you an answer that will be more than enough for you. I will give you a glimpse, a partial view." And so he adopts this device. He takes Moses to a rock and tells him to stand upon that rock. And then he says that while his glory is passing by he will put Moses in a cleft of the rock and cover him with his hand, but as he passes by he will take away his hand, and, he says to Moses, "Thou shalt see my back parts: but my face shall not be seen."

What is revival? It is just a glimpse of God's "back parts." It is just a sight of the glory of the eternal God. It is a glimpse of what awaits us all in the glory everlasting. And God, as he does this, pronounces his name, and he pronounces himself to be the sovereign Lord who says, "[I] will be gracious to whom I will be gracious, and will shew mercy on whom I will shew mercy." When revival comes, it humbles us. That is always the first thing. I believe our greatest need is to be humbled. We are much too healthy, much too confident, much too assured, much too bright and breezy. We need to be humbled to the dust and to be amazed at the power and the glory of God as we just see his back parts, as it were, passing by.

And the LORD passed by before him, and proclaimed, The LORD, The LORD God, merciful and gracious, longsuffering, and abundant in goodness and truth, keeping mercy for thousands, forgiving iniquity and transgression and sin, and that will by no means clear the guilty; visiting the iniquity of the fathers upon the children, and upon the children's children, unto the third and to the fourth generation. And Moses made haste, and bowed his head toward the earth, and worshipped. (Ex. 34:6–8)

And that is always the effect of revival. Its first effect is to humble us. We stop arguing, stop asking our questions, stop our self-justification, stop all our cleverness, and we are humbled and made to see that we are nothing. And then God pronounces the glorious truth and raises us up and sends us out.

Is this not what is needed today? We tend to forget God. We talk about him. We pray in a formal, perfunctory manner. Do we know anything about this pleading, this arguing, this reasoning, this interceding with God? The position is desperate, and nothing but some such action as this is adequate to it. What is the point of fighting rearguard actions in an age and in a day like this? There is only one thing that matters, and that is that we know this living, glorious God and have an experience of his power, his majesty, and his glory. And this is something that is possible to all of us.

I want to close this study with words preached by the great Charles Haddon Spurgeon in the year 1859 in London at the time of the great revival that started in America in 1857, came over to Britain in 1858, and reached Wales in 1859. Spurgeon was longing that it might happen in London. He knew about it personally, but his church did not, so he preached like this:

It is possible for a man to know whether God has called him or not. And he may know it beyond a doubt. He may know it as surely as if he had read it with his own eyes. Nay, he may know it more surely than if he had read it with his eyes. When I read a thing with mine eyes even my eyes may deceive me. The testimony of sense may be false. But the testimony of the Spirit must be true. We have this witness of the Spirit within, bearing witness with our spirits that we are born of God. There is such a thing on earth as an infallible assurance of our election. . . . What would some of you give if you could arrive at this assurance? Mark you, if you anxiously desire to know, you may know. If your heart pants to feel it, it shall do so ere long. No man ever desired Christ in his heart with a living and longing desire who did not find him sooner or later.

Then he goes on:

If thou hast a desire, God has given it thee. If thou pantest and criest and groanest after Christ, even this is his gift. Bless him for it. Thank him for little grace, and ask him for great grace. He has given thee hope; ask for faith. And when he gives thee faith; ask for assurance. And when thou gettest assurance, ask for full assurance. And when thou hast obtained full assurance, ask for enjoyment. And when thou hast enjoyment, ask for glory itself. And he shall surely give it thee, in his own appointed season.[8]

My dear good friends, do you feel the burden of the times? Are you grieved about the state of the church? Are you doing anything about it? There is a call today for those who feel the burden of these things and are concerned about the glory and the honor of the name of God and of Christ and of the church, to draw apart, to come together. Do not wait until everybody moves or you will never move. Get together. Seek the face of the Lord. Study his Word together, whatever denomination you belong to. The people of God seek him, they seek his face. Wait upon him. Wait for his answer. Above all, seek to have a glimpse of his glory, and then do what he tells you to do, and he will meet with you, and he will give you the blessing that you desire. And you will be used of him in leading others to a like knowledge of the truth. Oh, may God awaken in us the desire that was in the heart of Moses to know God and to have a glimpse of his glory.

O Lord, our God, we come to you again, and we thank you that we can do so. We know that you never refuse those who come to you with honest and contrite hearts and who truly seek your face. We bless your name that with you there is mercy, that you may be feared. We have all sinned. We have all fallen short. We have all been negligent. We are all too much at ease in Zion. O God, awaken us. Give us a true view of yourself and of your church and what you intend her to be. And, O Lord, create within us such a deep longing to see Zion clothed in her beautiful garments again, and a praise among the nations and the peoples, that we shall begin to intercede in this direction and not let you go until you have opened the windows of heaven and showered forth such a blessing that we shall scarcely be able to contain it. Lord, enlarge our minds, enlarge our hearts, in order that we may receive such blessings and then know that we shall run in the way of your commandments and be a praise unto the glory of your grace. And may the grace of the Lord Jesus Christ and the love of God and the fellowship and the communion of the Holy Spirit abide and continue with us now, throughout the remainder of this, our short, uncertain, earthly life and pilgrimage, until we shall see him as he is and be made like unto him in the glory everlasting. Amen.

8

THE NARROW WAY

☼

Enter ye in at the strait gate: for wide is the gate, and broad is the way, that leadeth to destruction, and many there be which go in thereat: because strait is the gate, and narrow is the way, which leadeth unto life, and few there be that find it.

MATTHEW 7:13–14

There is no charge, perhaps, that is brought quite so frequently against the Christian teaching, the Christian gospel, the Christian way of life, and the individual Christian believer as the charge of narrowness. It is said that we are mistaken, that we are dull and foolish, and so on. And this charge is brought against us particularly by the kind of man who, in his anxiety to show the breadth and the largeness of his own views, generally describes himself as being "a man of the world." He would have us see how broad his outlook is. Nothing less than a world dimension is wide enough and big enough to measure this outlook of his, in contradistinction to that narrow, cramped, confined person who calls himself a Christian.

But not only is that the favorite charge brought against us by people of the world, I am afraid that for many Christians there is no charge of which they are so nervous and frightened as this. They do not seem to mind that people say they are wrong or muddleheaded or traditionalist and so on. Anything, as long as it is not suggested that they are narrow. The average Christian seems to me to have a peculiar detestation of this particular charge. And, of course, there are certain senses in which that is a healthy and a right and true reaction. God forbid that any of us should ever really become narrow in the sense that the Pharisees were narrow—those legalists who would reduce the law and the grace of God to their petty little vetoes and restraints. God forbid that any of us should ever in this way reduce this glorious gospel of liberty to a mere number of prohibitions and foibles of our own. But that is not our danger at all. Our danger as modern Christians is really the exact opposite. It is that in our fear and dread and horror of being called narrow we could swing so far to the other extreme and in the end be so wide and so broad and so large that we lose our landmarks altogether and end by not knowing what the real meaning of the word *Christian* is. Everybody wants to claim a wide and a broad outlook. Breadth of understanding! A charity and a tolerance that is prepared to include everything! That seems, to me, to be the greatest danger.

Indeed, I sometimes think that a well-known story in *Aesop's Fables* has a great deal to say to many modern Christians. I am referring to the fable about the frog and the ox. The story is that one day there was a little frog in a field, and suddenly he happened to look up and saw this enormous creature standing by his side—the ox. This creature was so big, so great, so wide that as the little frog looked at him, he felt very small and cramped. After looking at the ox and admiring him, the frog began to be envious of him and then to feel he would like to become like the ox. Why should he not be big and great and broad also? So the little frog began to puff himself up, to inflate himself, and he blew and blew and blew until at last he became so big, so tall, and so wide that he just exploded and went out of existence. And that, unless I am very greatly mistaken, is precisely what seems to have happened to the so-called faith of many so-called Christians today. In their desire to be considered broad-minded, what little faith these Christians ever had has long since exploded and has gone out of existence.

But this not only applies to the individual. I believe the whole condition of the Christian church today is very largely due to this selfsame envy. The Christian church in her utter folly has been recognizing a new authority. This new authority, of course, is the man of knowledge, the man of culture, and particularly the man of scientific knowledge. And the church has been at great pains to do everything she can to please this new authority. This man of learning must never be offended. And in order to please him and to placate him, the church has been ready to reject things in the Bible. She throws out the first three chapters of Genesis in their entirety and much of the other history; she throws out all the miracles, including the miracles of our Lord; and she throws out the virgin birth, the incarnation, the atonement, and the literal, physical resurrection. In that way the church, and I am not exaggerating, has been prepared to trim and to clip and to change her message. She will throw out anything in order to make her teaching pleasing and acceptable to this new authority, the man of knowledge, the man of learning and culture, the man of science.

But in doing that, the church has departed very far indeed from the pattern and the example set for her by her Lord and Master. As I read the four Gospels, I never find the Lord Jesus Christ trimming and changing his gospel in order to make it suit the people. Rather, I find him trimming and clipping and changing the people in order to make them fit into his gospel. And, believe me, we shall see no revival, no new life in the church until we return to the royal manner and the royal pattern and example. The commission of every true preacher is this:

Ye servants of God, your Master proclaim,
And publish abroad his wonderful name.

CHARLES WESLEY

This is the truth that is committed unto us, and whatever people may say, whether they like it or whether they dislike it, we must preach it without fear and with a holy boldness.

Now I mention all that in order that I may say just a word in passing. If you are feeling a bit nervous about this charge of being called narrow, I would suggest that the next time one of these so-called "men of the world" comes to you and tells you that you are narrow-minded and cramped because you are a Christian, instead of apologizing, instead of trying to explain it away, instead of whimpering or running away, just stand your ground! Look such a person straight in the eye and say, "Of course I'm narrow. And it would be very much better for you, and especially for your wife and children, if you also became narrow and ceased to boast of a breadth and a largeness and a width that are nothing but an excuse for laxity and looseness and sin." Whatever else might happen, I can promise you this for certain: he will not worry you quite as frequently in the future as he has tended to do in the past!

However, that is an aside. What I am really concerned to do here is to consider this narrowness. The remarkable thing is that when our Lord Jesus Christ came to choose a name or a designation for his kingdom and for his way of life, he deliberately chose this word of which you and I tend to be so nervous. Had you ever thought of that? He has the vocabulary of the whole universe at his disposal, and yet when he comes to name his way of life, he deliberately calls it "the narrow way." The thing that you and I are a little bit ashamed of, he boasts of. He exults in and puts on the flag of the kingdom: the "strait gate," "the narrow way." He glories in the thing that so alarms and terrifies us.

Why is this? Why did our Lord deliberately choose to call his way of life "the narrow way"? He never did anything by accident or haphazardly. When, therefore, he gives this name to his way of life, he has very good reasons. What are they? Why should we call his way "the narrow way"? Why should we walk on it? Why should we glory and exult in this narrowness? Or, to put my question differently, in what respects is it true to say of the Christian way of life that it is indeed the narrow way?

The first respect in which this way of life is narrow is that it deliberately confines the field of its considerations to one subject. Now this is remarkable. The gospel starts by being narrow. It narrows down even the very things it is going to consider. This is, of course, very surprising, particularly to people today. We are living in the age of encyclopedias, are we not? And in an encyclopedia you find a little bit of knowledge about many, many subjects. That is the characteristic of this age. We have a tabloid mentality. We want to know a little bit of information about everything. But that is the exact opposite of what we have here.

Take this book the Bible, the great old book of sixty-six books, written at different times by different people in different circumstances. In this book there is a great variety of subjects. There is much about creation and history; there is much about births and marriages and deaths and wars. And yet this book is not an encyclopedia. It is a very specialized book. It is the manual of the soul. This book has only one theme from beginning to end, and that one theme is God and man, or man in his relationship to the eternal God. It is not a book that tells you a little about many things. It is a book that tells you everything about that one central theme, and it keeps itself to that. It is a specialist book.

And what is true of the book is true of the Master of the book. If ever there was a specialist in this world, it was the Lord Jesus Christ. Look at the things he might have done. Look at the ability, the knowledge, at his command. Yet he deliberately keeps himself to one theme. Had you ever noticed that as you read the four Gospels? There is a sense in which it is true to say that the Lord Jesus Christ had only one sermon, and he went on preaching that one sermon for three years. He varied his illustrations, but there was only one point. And that one essential sermon was about this whole question of the human soul in its relationship to the everlasting God.

Let me illustrate what I mean. Here is our Lord one afternoon in the country with his followers, and he sees a farmer sowing the seed on the ground. Now it is quite clear that our Lord knew a good deal about agriculture and was interested in it, but the sight of that farmer does not lead our Lord to give a lecture on agriculture. Our Lord never lectured; he always preached. This is how he puts it: "Do you see that farmer?" he says in effect. "He's sowing seed, yes. But incidentally he's doing another thing. He's testing the ground. There's only one type of seed, but there are many types of ground, and the ground will be judged by its response to the seed that the farmer is sowing. You know," our Lord says, "I am like that farmer. What is my preaching? It's nothing but the sowing of the word of life. And as I'm preaching to you, I'm testing you. You will be judged in eternity by your response to my preaching, to the words that I'm speaking to you. Take heed how you hear." And our Lord concludes, "He that hath ears to hear, let him hear" (Mark 4:3–9).

Then on another occasion our Lord is out in the country again, but this time he is standing opposite an orchard, and the trees in the orchard are bearing various kinds of fruit. Our Lord looks at the orchard, and again he is obviously interested in horticulture, but the sight of the orchard does not make him give an address on horticulture. No, no! He sees another illustration of his one point. This time he says in effect, "Look at those trees. How do you judge a tree? You judge it by the fruit that it bears, which may be good or bad. Have you realized that you are like those trees and that in this world you are bearing fruit and it can be good or bad?" And he says, "Ye shall know them by their fruits" (Matt. 7:16–18). You are going to be judged in eternity by the fruit that you bear in this life. It is exactly the same point but illustrated in a different way.

And then another illustration. Our Lord is in the country again, and he looks at the birds flying in the air and the flowers, "the lilies of the field." Does that send him home to write poems about flowers or to try to paint birds? Of course not! Our Lord was not interested in art for art's sake. He just sees another illustration for the same point. He says in essence, "If God so clothes the lily, if God is so interested in the birds of the air, how much greater is his interest in you, you everlasting souls?" (Matt. 6:26–30).

All the vast knowledge that our Lord has and commands, he simply uses to illustrate or to bring out the point that there is only one thing that matters in this world, and that is the soul and its relationship to God. Not a word of politics, not a word of protest against the Roman authorities that have conquered them. No, no! Just one theme, and he narrows it down to this—the soul of man. He sums it up in a tremendous word: "For what shall it profit a man, if he shall gain the whole world"—of wealth and knowledge and everything—"and lose his own soul? Or what shall a man give in exchange for his soul?" (Mark 8:36–37). This is the one thing he is interested in.

But our Lord even narrows that down. That is very narrow, as judged by the modern mentality, but our Lord is not only interested in the soul as an idea and as a concept—he is interested in the individual soul, in the personal soul. He narrows it down. And that was the big difference between our Lord's interest in the soul and the interest of the Greek philosophers, who had lived and died before Jesus ever came into the world. The Greek philosophers were interested in the soul, yes, but always as an idea, as a thought, as some vague concept. That was not our Lord's interest. He was interested in the personal soul, the individual soul, your soul, my soul. And that is why many modern persons dislike this gospel so intensely and will say, "All right, when you were talking about the soul, I was interested and I was in agreement, but now you're getting personal. You're bringing it down to me. You're talking about me. This is intolerable."

That is exactly like one of the prime ministers in Great Britain in the nineteenth century, Lord Melbourne, who happened to be prime minister when Queen Victoria came to the throne. He was a member of the Church of England, but a formalist. He went to church now and again, paid lip service, was supposedly a Christian. But he betrayed himself on one occasion when he put it like this: "Things are coming to a pretty pass if religion's going to start being personal." Religion is all right when you have some great state occasion, when there is a coronation or a royal death or the funeral of a president. Religion then is very good. It adds a little bit of dignity and ceremony. But if religion is going to interfere in my personal life and living, it becomes intolerable.

But the Lord Jesus Christ was always personal. He was intensely personal. Let me give you but one illustration to prove my point. You find it in the fourth chapter of the Gospel according to John, in the famous story of our Lord's meeting with the so-called woman of Samaria. One afternoon he was too tired to go with the disciples to the neighboring town to buy provisions, and he sat down by the side of a well to have a rest. Scarcely had he done so than this woman came to draw water from the well. And the moment she came, they began to have a discussion. What was it about? It was about religion. What were the topics? Who did this well belong to—the Jews or the Samaritans? Another question: Where should you worship—on this mountain, or were the Jews right in saying you could only worship in the temple in Jerusalem? On she went to her heart's content.

Obviously an able woman, clever, subtle at the art of repartee, the woman of Samaria was enjoying this discussion immensely, until our Lord did something that no modern gentleman would ever dream of doing. He became personal. Fancy becoming personal in an argument about religion! But he did. He suddenly turned to this woman and said, "Go, call thy husband, and come hither," to which the woman said, "I have no husband." And our Lord replied, "Thou hast well said, I have no husband: for thou hast had five husbands; and he whom thou now hast is not thy husband" (John 4:16–18). In other words, he revealed that he knew all about the life of sin and adultery that she was living at that very moment. In effect he said to her, "My dear good woman, you were talking cleverly and glibly and giving your opinion on God, on heaven and hell and worship and all these matters of religion. And in the meantime, look at your own life. Put yourself right first, and then perhaps you may have a right to express your opinion. Start with yourself." That was our Lord's method.

But to modern men and women this is hateful. It is abominable. "Oh, of course, discussion on religion is always good, isn't it? If there's nothing else to talk about, we can always have a discussion about religion!" And we give our opinions about God and what God ought to be doing and what we think of this and that. And in the meantime we are neglecting our own lives and manner of living and ignoring our sinning and unworthiness. We cannot even control ourselves, but we will express our opinion on the cosmos and on the mind of God!

But our Lord Jesus Christ will not allow us to do that. He is not interested in our opinions. They are utterly irrelevant. The one thing he tells each of us to be concerned about is our own soul, our relationship to God. And this is something that is intensely personal. He talks about entering into a "strait gate," and I always think that this strait gate is not like the gate in the pictures that old people used to hang on their walls. I think this "strait gate" is a turnstile. And the point about a turnstile is that it only admits one person at a time. Two cannot go together through a turnstile. Husband and wife cannot go together. Father and mother cannot go together. Parents and children must go through the turnstile one by one. That is the "strait gate": you and God. Your parents may be the most saintly people anyone has ever known. That does not save you. Each one of us must come to a private, personal, individual meeting with God. We cannot ride into heaven on the backs of saintly ancestors. We cannot be saved in nations or churches or towns or districts or communities. Each of us has to come alone, face-to- face with God. This is personal! Our Lord narrows it down to this.

"The eyes of a fool," says the Old Testament, "are in the ends of the earth" (Prov. 17:24). People are talking today about the war in Vietnam and this and the other problem, and the church is talking about all these things, and people are saying that God ought to do this and that. My dear friend, those are not the questions. The question is, do you know God? What is your personal relationship to God? Our Lord invites us to come back to our own doorsteps and face God individually and alone. He narrows it down to that.

But having done that, our Lord narrows it still further. Having said that faith is an intensely personal matter, he then goes on to insist upon dictating the way in which we live. And that, of course, is the great theme of the Sermon on the Mount, as we call it, and Matthew 7:13–14 is the beginning of a kind of epilogue to that sermon. Our Lord dictates, I say, the way in which we live.

"Ah, yes," says the modern man, "that's why I hate it. Your gospel is so narrow. It tells me what I mustn't do and tells me what I must do. It interferes with my liberty as a human being. It's impossibly narrow. It's too cramped. It's too confined. Give me something big and great. Give me a large view."

People hate the ethical emphasis of the Scriptures and especially of the gospel. But whether we like it or not, this is a fact. Our Lord does do this. He dictates the way in which we live both negatively and positively. Negatively, the gospel is summed up perfectly for us in the second half of the Ten Commandments. Here is how the gospel tells us we are to live:

- Thou shalt not kill.
- Thou shalt not commit adultery.
- Thou shalt not steal.
- Thou shalt not bear false witness against your neighbor.
- You must not covet your neighbor's house, you must not covet your neighbor's wife or his manservant or his maidservant or his ox or his donkey or anything that is your neighbor's (see Ex. 20:13–17).

That is the negative aspect of this ethical teaching of the Scriptures.

"Oh," says the modern man, "I object to these prohibitions, these vetoes!"

I agree with you—it is narrow. But have you ever realized that if only everybody in the world today were as narrow as this gospel would have us be, there would be no war? There would be no drunkenness, no infidelity or separations or divorces. There would be no heartbreak among little children, nor all the suffering of the world. If only everybody in the world today lived according to the Ten Commandments and the negative aspects of the Sermon on the Mount, the world would be paradise. The problems would vanish. And therein we see the folly of this objection to the narrowness of the gospel. If you like, it is the narrowness that is characteristic of God himself, for we are told, "[God is] the Father of lights, with whom is no variableness, neither shadow of turning" (James 1:17). "God," says Paul to Titus, ". . . cannot lie" (Titus 1:2). "God," says James, "cannot be tempted with evil, neither tempteth he any man" (James 1:13). God is constrained by his own utter, absolute holiness, and sin and evil are impossible to him.

Oh, that we would all begin to seek and to covet this narrowness instead of boasting of a breadth and a width and a largeness of outlook that leads to moral and political and social and international chaos— the horrors of which we are so aware in our modern world. That is the negative narrowness of the Sermon on the Mount. But look at the positive narrowness. It is even more wonderful. "Enter ye in at the strait gate," says our Lord. He bids us to come into the narrow way. I think he is saying something like this—this is a part of the Sermon on the Mount: "Come with me to the mountaintop. Don't be content to live life anyhow, somehow on the dull plains of life. Anybody can do that. Come up to the heights."

In other words, the narrowness that I find here is what we may well call the narrowness of circles. Have you ever thought of this? The higher you go through ascending circles, the fewer people you find in each circle. We all belong to society in general, but the number of people who are intimate with the American president or the British queen is small.

In social circles, the higher you go, the fewer people are in your circle. It is true of every profession or walk of life. The higher you rise, the fewer your competitors. Whether it is singing or art or music, the higher the circle of achievement, the fewer people you will find in it. That is the invitation that our Lord is giving. Come, he says, up to the heights. Do not be content just to shuffle through this world and through life. Come after me, he says, scale the heights. Let us ascend to the topmost summit of this mountain.

And here is the real meaning: "Be ye therefore perfect, even as your Father which is in heaven is perfect" (Matt. 5:48). Come to the top of the mountain. Do not live as any fool can live. It is easy to float out when the tide is going out or to float downstream. It is easy to get drunk and go wrong. Any fool can do that; every fool is doing that. Our Lord says: Do not do that. Be exceptional. Be great. Be like God. Come to the topmost circle, in which is God himself. "Be ye therefore perfect, even as your Father which is in heaven is perfect." That is the narrowness.

And that brings me to my last point. The narrowness of the gospel is finally seen in this: that having said all that, our Lord then goes on to say that salvation and deliverance from our estranged position, estranged from God and under the condemnation of God and his holy law, is only possible for us through one person. And our Lord even narrows that. It is through that one person crucified—"Jesus Christ, and him crucified" (1 Cor. 2:2).

"Yes," says the modern man, "that's exactly why I've left the church. I have no interest in it whatsoever. You narrow Christians, you don't know anything about Confucius and Buddha and Mohammed and the great Greek philosophers. You restrict yourselves to one book and just one person, and you say it's Jesus Christ alone, and you're not interested in wide thinking and broad outlooks, and then you say that I have to believe that one person could die to atone for the sin of the whole world—propitiation for the sin of the world. It's impossible. It's ridiculous. One dying for another? One being punished who's innocent and the others being saved? Absurd."

So people reject the cross. They pour scorn and derision upon it, upon faith in Jesus Christ alone and his death in particular. What do we have to say to such people? Well, we do not argue with them. The gospel does not argue. It is more of a challenge than an argument. It is a proclamation. And what the gospel says to such a person is this: My dear friend, if you can find God and know him without going through Jesus Christ and him crucified, good luck to you! If you can live a successful and worthy life in a world like this without getting any help from him, I have nothing to do but to congratulate you, to admire you and to envy you. If you can arrive on your deathbed or stand over an open grave without fear or terror or hesitation or doubt and feel you are ready to stand before the everlasting and eternal God in judgment, again I can but tell you to carry on.

But if ever you feel you are lost and forlorn, if ever you feel that you are a miserable failure, if ever you realize that you do not know God and confess it, if ever you realize you are afraid of death and are not ready to meet it and that if you did stand before God you would have nothing to say, if ever it all comes back to you and you are stripped naked and you have nothing and you see yourself in utter hopelessness and desperation and final despair, turn back to him, the Christ you have rejected and whose voice you have spurned, the Christ of the cross. And you will find him still there, and he will not refuse you. He will still be ready to receive you, though you make of him the last resort of a desperate sinner. That is the message. When everything else has failed you, turn to him, the Christ of Calvary, the one through whom God was reconciling the world unto himself, and he will receive you, take away your fears, and give you the assurance that he has borne your punishment. He will reconcile you and introduce you to God and open the gate into heaven. That is the narrowness of the gospel.

Let me put it to you like this. Have you ever noticed, I wonder, that the earthly life and course of our blessed Lord himself is *the* perfect commentary on my text? Here it is. "Strait is the gate, and narrow is the way," but it "leadeth unto life." Look at it like this. Take his coming into this world, take his birth in Bethlehem. Was there ever such "straitening"? "Strait is the gate." "Strait" means narrow. Was there ever such a narrowing? There is the eternal Son of God—coequal, coeternal with his Father—but he is born! He comes as a helpless babe. Oh, the narrowing that took place at Bethlehem!

But watch him as he goes along. See him in his life. See him, especially, setting out on his earthly ministry. Keep your eye on the Pharisees and the scribes and the Sadducees. Watch them spreading around him and gradually drawing in—the trick questions they put to him. They are narrowing him down. "Strait is the gate . . . narrow is the way."

Come along. Look at him in a garden called Gethsemane. Remember, this is the one who created the whole universe. They have confined him now to a garden. Soldiers surround the garden. He is allowed to walk up and down the garden, but he cannot go outside. "Strait is the gate . . . narrow is the way."

They are narrowing him down. They are closing in on him, and, indeed, look at him in a few hours. He is now under arrest with a soldier on one side and a soldier on the other. He cannot walk backwards and forward now. He can move his hands and his legs, if he chooses, but he cannot move about. They have narrowed him down. The soldiers are hemming him in.

What am I talking about? Look at him on the cross, the Creator of the world, the Lord of life, nailed to a tree. He cannot move his hands or feet. They have fixed him. They have brought him down to this. He is immovable. Crucified. Nailed to the tree. "Strait is the gate . . . narrow is the way."

And he dies. They take down his body, and they put it into a tomb. Look into that tomb. Do the very sides not seem to collapse? It is the end. "Strait is the gate . . . narrow is the way."

Bethlehem. Enemies. Persecutions. Trials. Agony. Sweating blood in the garden. Trial. Condemnation. Crucifixion. Death. Burial. Tomb. "Strait is the gate, and narrow is the way." And it leads to the grave. But, thank God, my text does not stop there. "Strait is the gate . . . narrow is the way"—but it "leadeth unto life." So it does. Bethlehem. Enemies. Opposition. Trial. Reviling. Agony and sweat. Trial. Condemnation. Crucifixion. Death. Burial. Tomb. But he burst asunder the bands of death, arose triumphant over the grave, "and hath brought life and immortality to light through the gospel" (2 Tim. 1:10).

There it is, my dear friends, all in this marvelous picture of our Lord's coming and going. The one thing that matters is that we should all know of a surety that we have entered this "strait gate" and that we are this moment on the narrow way. Oh, the madness of the world! "Ah," it says, "the narrowness! It's too cramped. Impossible." And the world goes the other way. But look at what our Lord says about the other way: "Wide is the gate, and broad is the way." Look at them, the thousands, drinking, dancing, singing, indulging in sex, taking drugs, spitting on holy things. "Life," they say, "is marvelous! Look at the crowd."

Yes, look at the crowd. The vital question to ask about a path is not so much about its width as its destination. "Wide is the gate, and broad is the way"—but where does it lead?—"that leadeth to destruction." It is already the destruction of everything that is best in human nature. Look at the violence these poor young people are doing to all their highest and best qualities. The first qualities to suffer from drink and drugs are always the higher centers, the best qualities—sensitivity, refinement, understanding, chastity, purity. These are the things that go first. And it ends in destruction.

The other way seems very narrow at the beginning, does it not? There are not many people on it. But consider, says our Lord, where it is going to bring you. "Strait is the gate." You seem at first to be having to give up things to become a Christian. But it is the biggest folly to think that. That appears to be the case because we are blinded by sin. But actually when you enter in at the strait gate, you begin to walk on the narrow way, and you see him ahead of you. And our Lord has everything. All the treasures of God's wisdom and riches and grace are in him. He gives you everything. The very hairs of your head are all numbered. He showers his grace upon you. There is nothing that you can ever need but that he will give it to you. With the apostle Paul, you will be able to say, "I have learned, in whatsoever state I am, therewith to be content. I know both how to be abased, and I know how to abound. . . . I can do all things through Christ which strengtheneth me" (Phil. 4:11–13). You are in the company of Christ and of the saints, and you go on and on. "Strait is the gate, and narrow is the way." But it "leadeth unto life," life that is life indeed, life more abundant, the life of God, the life of eternal bliss.

My dear friend, where are you? You are on one or the other of these two ways. If you are not certain that you are on this narrow way, here is the invitation now. Enter in, just as you are, by the strait gate. Come onto the narrow way.

O Lord our God, we thank you for this glorious gospel. We thank you that it is as it is. We thank you that it is not of human invention. We thank you that it is essentially different from everything else in the world. Lord, we bless your name for this, for its holiness, its purity, its cleanliness, for everything in it that makes us realize the dignity of manhood and of womanhood and restores to us in its original manner the image that has become so marred in us all by nature, as children of Adam and children of the fall. O Lord, have mercy and have pity upon all who, controlled in their thinking by this foolish mind of the world, regard such a glorious gospel as narrow. Lord, enable them to see that this is life that is life indeed, life more abundant, glorious life. Lord, open the eyes of the blind. Hear us in the name of your dear Son, our Lord and Savior Jesus Christ. Amen.

9

A NEW AND
LIVING WAY

✸

> Having therefore, brethren, boldness to enter into the holiest by the blood of Jesus, by a new and living way, which he hath consecrated for us, through the veil, that is to say, his flesh; and having an high priest over the house of God; let us draw near with a true heart in full assurance of faith, having our hearts sprinkled from an evil conscience, and our bodies washed with pure water.
>
> HEBREWS 10:19–22

We are dealing here with one of the exhortations found in the great epistle of Hebrews. This is an epistle written to people who are described as Hebrews. That means that they were Jews, people who had been brought up in the Jewish religion but who, having heard the Christian message, believed it and espoused it and became members of the Christian church.

One gathers that for a time these Hebrew Christians had rejoiced in their salvation. But now, for a number of reasons, they had become discouraged. They had been subjected, as verses 32–34 of this very chapter remind us, to a good deal of persecution, and as a result they had become not only discouraged but even doubtful, uncertain, and hesitant concerning their faith. And it is obvious that some were even beginning to look back to the old Jewish religion and to the temple and its ceremonies, feeling that perhaps they had been a little hasty in taking up this new teaching and forsaking an old religion that had stood the test of centuries. So it is obvious that they were in a very dangerous condition, and the whole object of this epistle is to warn them against the terrible danger of apostasy, of turning away from the Christian faith. The method that the writer adopts is to put before them the greatness and the glories of the gospel and to show them the consequences of turning away from it. And he does this in various ways, applying his message along various lines.

In the verses that we are considering, the writer shows these Hebrew Christians the importance of doctrine from the standpoint of prayer. That is what he is dealing with here—"boldness to enter into the holiest." A Christian cannot live without prayer. Our Lord himself taught us that "men ought always to pray, and not to faint" (Luke 18:1). If we do not pray, we shall faint. Prayer is absolutely essential to the life of the Christian. But the main question is, how is this to be done? It is one thing to talk about prayer; it is a very different thing to pray. And here the writer teaches us the only way whereby we can pray truly, because, you notice, he says that we are not only to pray, we are to pray with "boldness," with confidence, with assurance, and he uses the term, "full assurance of faith." Prayer is not some vague crying out for help to any powers that may be; it is a confidence and an assurance and a bold approach to God. And without this, as the writer teaches, the Christian cannot continue. That was true in the first century, and it is true today. We are surrounded by problems and difficulties and perplexities, and nothing is more important for us than that we should know exactly how we are to pray. Let me put a question to you before I go any further: do you pray with boldness, with assurance, with certainty, with complete confidence? That is true prayer.

So now let us see what this writer has to tell us about genuine prayer. And it seems to me that the first point is that there are real difficulties with regard to this matter of prayer. I have often felt that if we have never realized these difficulties, it is probable that we have never prayed at all. And yet today there is a teaching, which is very popular, that would have us believe that prayer is the simplest thing in the world. This is something we are being told constantly in connection with conferences concerning unity and ecumenicity. They do not talk about doctrine. In their view, doctrine divides us. But, they say, there is one thing we can always do: we can always pray together. There was a teaching a few years ago that went as far as to say that prayer is like breathing, and all you need to do is sit in a comfortable chair and relax in it and just begin to listen to God and speak to him.

People think that prayer is simple, and yet I want to try to show you that according to the biblical teaching, prayer is extremely difficult, perhaps the most difficult thing of all in the Christian life. Surely every preacher will agree with me when I say that it is very much easier to preach than it is to pray. Prayer has real difficulties, and the people who have never realized that have probably never prayed.

What are these difficulties? Well, notice the ones that the writer suggests here. The first thing about prayer, and the thing that, in a way, makes it completely impossible for us, is that it means entering into the holiest, the holiest of all: "Having therefore, brethren, boldness to enter into the *holiest* by the blood of Jesus." As I have stated, the author of this epistle is writing to Hebrew Christians, and he is using a term with which they were very familiar. He is referring, of course, to the temple, and the tabernacle before that, and the structure of those buildings.

The area outside the temple building was divided into a number of courts; there was an outer court into which anybody could enter, and there was a court for the Jews and another court into which the priests alone were allowed. Within the temple there was a "veil" or curtain, on the other side of which was a place called "the holiest of all." This was a place into which only one man was allowed to go; even the priests were not allowed to enter. That one man was the high priest. And he was allowed to enter only once a year. Why was this? The answer is that in the holiest of all, this innermost sanctum, was the presence of God. There was a glory there, the Shekinah glory. In Solomon's temple, the ark of the covenant was there, with its lid or mercy seat, on which were the two cherubim, and inside the ark the tables of the law. It was there that God came and met the representative of the people, the high priest.

We do not talk to ourselves when we pray. We do not talk to other people. To pray means to enter into the very presence of God. That is why not only is prayer difficult, but when you realize something of what prayer means, it appears at first sight to be completely impossible. "Who among us shall dwell with the devouring fire?" asks Isaiah (Isa. 33:14).

Who can dwell in the presence of this burning light? "God is light, and in him is no darkness at all" (1 John 1:5). Now the writer is so concerned about this that he comes back to the same point again, at the end of the twelfth chapter. He seems to have an aversion to Christians who think that the mark of spirituality is familiarity with God and an easy glibness in prayer. This is how he puts it: "Wherefore we receiving a kingdom which cannot be moved, let us have grace, whereby we may serve God acceptably with reverence and godly fear: for our God is a consuming fire" (Heb. 12:28–29). Now the moment you begin to realize something about that, you begin to feel, I repeat, that prayer is quite impossible. How can anyone enter into the presence of such a Being? How can anyone be just with such a God? Here is the first big difficulty, the first great obstacle. But let me hurry to the second.

The second great difficulty, always, with prayer is what the author calls here "an evil conscience." In verse 22 he says, "Let us draw near with a true heart in full assurance of faith, having our hearts sprinkled from an evil conscience." We can talk to people, and we can justify ourselves before them. There is no difficulty about that. We are all very good at balancing the accounts. Whatever charge anybody may bring against us, we always have an answer. But the moment you turn to God in prayer, your conscience begins to speak; it is within you, and you cannot silence it. It produces facts and lays them before you. And do what you will, you cannot answer that voice of conscience. There are many great illustrations of this in the various parts of the Scriptures.

Perhaps one of the most notable examples is that of David, the king of Israel. It is described for us most powerfully in Psalm 51. David was guilty of two terrible sins—he committed adultery and then murder. And he was very pleased with himself until, through the prophet Nathan, his conscience began to speak to him, and then he was in terrible trouble. "Have mercy upon me, O God," he says, "according to thy lovingkindness: according unto the multitude of thy tender mercies blot out my transgressions" (v. 1). There is no defense. "Against thee, thee only, have I sinned, and done this evil in thy sight" (v. 4). "For I acknowledge my transgressions: and my sin is ever before me" (v. 3).

The accusations of conscience, "an evil conscience," wake up your past sins, parading them before you; your conscience will not allow you to turn away or avert your gaze. This is the terrible problem of conscience.

It was the same with the prodigal son, a man who had justified himself, who was proud of himself. At last he came to himself and saw his sin, and he went back to his father. He had no defense. He had sinned against heaven and against his father and was no longer worthy to be called his father's son (Luke 15:11–19).

Unless you can deal with the conscience, you do not really pray, for you spend all your time on your knees arguing with yourself and trying somehow to deal with the accusations of conscience. While you are doing that, you are not praying. There is the second great difficulty.

And then we come to the third and the last of the great difficulties that the writer puts before us, and that is a sense of uncleanness: ". . . and our bodies washed with pure water." In other words, the ultimate problem about prayer is not simply the guilt of sin but the pollution of sin, the feeling that we are totally unworthy in and of ourselves, which is the problem with any actions we may or may not have performed. Here is the ultimate problem. How can a man or woman, whose nature is evil and sinful and wrong, ever enter into the presence of this holy God? And here again is what David expresses so perfectly in that fifty-first psalm. For David very soon comes to the realization that the real trouble with him, the real problem, is not so much that he has committed adultery and then murder, but that he ever desired to do these things, that his struggle is not so much his action as his heart, this evil, polluted, foul nature that ever created within him the desire to do these things. So he cries out in his agony, "Wash me throughly from mine iniquity, and cleanse me from my sin" (v. 2).

Here is my trouble, says David. "I was shapen in iniquity; and in sin did my mother conceive me" (v. 5). "Thou desirest truth in the inward parts" (v. 6). Not like the Pharisees, who only dealt with the outward parts, the outside of the cup and the platter. David knows that God looks upon the heart, for as our Lord put it to the Pharisees, "Ye are they which justify yourselves before men; but God knoweth your hearts: for that

165

which is highly esteemed among men is abomination in the sight of God" (Luke 16:15). God sees the heart! "In the hidden part thou shalt make me to know wisdom" (Ps. 51:6). So David cries out, "Purge me with hyssop, and I shall be clean: wash me, and I shall be whiter than snow" (v. 7). And then comes the real prayer: "Create in me a clean heart, O God; and renew a right spirit within me" (v. 10). This is the problem, this pollution of evil. The prodigal son said to his father, "And [I] am no more worthy to be called thy son: make me as one of thy hired servants" (Luke 15:19). He was saying, "I can manage that, but I've lost the right to be called your son. My nature is vile and foul; I'm rotten."

Here, then, are the three great difficulties and obstacles in connection with prayer. And my contention is that we have never prayed at all unless we have realized these three problems and have overcome them. And that is what the writer does here. He assures us of the only way whereby they can be overcome. And, thank God, here it is, and here is the gospel. But he is particularly concerned that these people should understand this. They thought they could still go on praying after forsaking the doctrine. His whole object is to show them that without right doctrine prayer is impossible. So he goes on to tell them the only way whereby we can ever really pray. What are the essentials?

The first is, we must have *a true heart*. "Let us draw near," the writer says, "with a true heart." That means sincerity. That means honesty. You cannot dissemble before God; you cannot mislead God. He sees and knows all things. This man keeps on repeating that point. He puts it like this in chapter 4:

> For the word of God is quick, and powerful, and sharper than any twoedged sword, piercing even to the dividing asunder of soul and spirit, and of the joints and marrow, and is a discerner of the thoughts and intents of the heart. Neither is there any creature that is not manifest in his sight: but all things are naked and opened unto the eyes of him with whom we have to do. (vv. 12–13)

We can fool people, but we will never fool God. He knows all about us. So it is absolutely essential that we have a true heart. We must be honest. We must be open. Again the psalmist has said it: "If I regard [or conceal] iniquity in my heart, the Lord will not hear me" (Ps. 66:18). If you are harboring or hiding something, God will not listen to you. He demands this absolute honesty and openness before him. That is essential.

And yet even that is not enough. You can be quite sincere, but that does not guarantee that you will have an entrance into the presence of God, that you will be truly praying, or that your prayer will be accepted. Other things, this writer says, are equally essential. What are they? "Having therefore, brethren, boldness to enter into the holiest by the blood of Jesus, by a new and living way, which he hath consecrated for us, through the veil, that is to say, his flesh; and having an high priest over the house of God; let us draw near" (vv. 19–22). So, then, how can we pray? The answer is that there is *"a new . . . way."* This is what the writer is emphasizing. Notice how he draws out and works out the contrast. These foolish Hebrew Christians were beginning to look back to the old way. There they were, Christian people, looking back to the temple and its worship and its ceremonies and to the earthly priesthood, and the author is amazed at them. He says in effect, "You are looking back at the old because you don't realize the glories and the perfection of the new way."

The writer is holding out before these Hebrew Christians this new way, and it is part of his great argument in this epistle. He contrasts the old covenant with the new, the temple worship with spiritual Christian worship, and he draws out these mighty contrasts. It is a new way. We must remember that it is a way that was planned in eternity, even before the creation of the world. But it is new in the sense that it has only just been put into operation, and that is in Christ Jesus.

Then the writer takes up his second point of contrast, which is that it is *"a . . . living way."* What does he mean by this? Well, he has been telling us as he has been working out this argument. He has pointed out that the characteristic of the old way was that it was dependent upon an earthly priesthood. So we read:

> Then said he, Lo, I come to do thy will, O God. He taketh away the first, that he may establish the second. By the which will we are sanctified through the offering of the body of Jesus Christ once for all. And every priest standeth daily ministering and offering oftentimes the same

> sacrifices, which can never take away sins: but this man, after he had offered one sacrifice for sins for ever, sat down on the right hand of God; from henceforth expecting till his enemies be made his footstool. (Heb. 10:9–13)

The point of contrast is this: there was a deadness about that old way; there was no life in it. It was dependent upon the earthly priesthood, but those priests got old, and they died, and others came. And that applied to the high priest as well as to the ordinary priests—a coming and a going. But here is one who has done something once and forever, and he lives evermore. The writer says all this in chapter 7:

> By so much was Jesus made a surety of a better testament. And they truly were many priests, because they were not suffered to continue by reason of death: but this man, because he continueth ever, hath an unchangeable priesthood. Wherefore he is able also to save them to the uttermost that come unto God by him, seeing he ever liveth to make intercession for them. (vv. 22–25)

No longer that old dead way, but the living way. And the writer exhorts these people. He says in effect, "Why are you looking back at the old way? You're mad to go back to the old, the dead, the passing, the temporal when you have the new, the living, and the eternal."

Do you see the importance and the relevance of all this to the present time? There arc people today, Christian people, who seem to want to go back to the old way. They are returning to an earthly, human priesthood, to ceremonies and rituals that have been replaced because they were inadequate. They are turning their backs on the new and living and eternal way that is in Christ Jesus. We modern people ought to understand this teaching quite well. We have great highways today. We want to get quickly from one place to another, and we no longer have to go meandering through the streets of a town. We bypass it. That is what the writer is talking about. No longer all that ritual and ceremony and the passing, human, dead element but rather one clear, new way in Christ Jesus, the Son of God, a new and living way.

Then the writer goes on to tell us about the characteristics of this marvelous new way. Again we ought to understand this in a real manner in these modern times. One of the most important things about our new highways is that they have good, solid foundations. They have to carry a lot of traffic, and unless they have good foundations we will soon be in trouble. The basis, the foundation, is so important. It is the same in the Christian life. And the author of this epistle tells us what that foundation is. He says that this "new and living way" has been "consecrated for us, through the veil, that is to say, his flesh" (Heb. 10:20). He has already been telling us what this means. This new way is built upon the foundation of the incarnation: "Wherefore when he cometh into the world, he saith, Sacrifice and offering thou wouldest not, but a body hast thou prepared me" (v. 5). This is what makes prayer possible. The Lord Jesus Christ came into the world, in a sense, in order that we might pray. There is only one way of access to God. Jesus said, "I am the way, the truth, and the life: no man cometh unto the Father, but by me" (John 14:6). So you need the basis of the incarnation. Two natures in the one person. It is the only foundation that is big and solid enough to take the traffic that goes along it to God and into his immediate presence.

But there is more to this than the incarnation. The writer has already referred to the blood of Jesus and to an offering, and here, of course, is the essence of it all. The incarnation alone would not have enabled us to go into the presence of God. Something more was necessary. And that was that our sin should be dealt with, that our guilt should be dealt with. And Jesus Christ did it: "Who his own self bare our sins in his own body on the tree" (1 Pet. 2:24). His body was broken. His blood was shed. Reconciliation has been established by the blood of Jesus. This is the way. It is the only way. There is no real entrance into the presence of God except by this "new and living way." He has passed through the heavens, and he is now "an high priest over the house of God" (v. 21).

You see, you cannot pray without having right doctrine. You cannot pray without the doctrines of the incarnation, the life of perfect obedience, the atoning substitution, the sacrificial death, the literal resurrection, the ascension, the heavenly session. All these are absolutely essential. You can talk to yourself, but you cannot talk to God. Prayer means entering into the holiest of all. And there is our Lord, who "ever liveth to make intercession for [us]" (Heb. 7:25).

The writer to the Hebrews says this is the way—the only way—whereby we can ever pray truly. Is this sufficient? This is the question. These Hebrew Christians had become doubtful about it. That was why they were turning back. But he wants them to have true assurance of faith, absolute certainty. So we must ask the question: Is this new and living way sufficient? Is it adequate? Does it enable me to go to God with a holy boldness? There is a kind of paradox here. On the one hand, he tells us that we must approach God "with reverence and godly fear: for our God is a consuming fire" (Heb. 12:28–29), and yet he tells us to go with "boldness" and with "full assurance of faith." How is this possible?

The writer has already given us the answer. Here is the only solution to the three problems that I put before you at the beginning of this study. To enter into the holiest of all, to come face-to-face with God, is this way adequate? And there is only one answer. It is God's own way. It is God who planned it. God was the engineer, as it were. He planned it before the very dawn of history. God worked out this way, the only way, in that eternal counsel between Father, Son, and Holy Spirit. It is God's own way, which makes Paul, in writing to the Romans, say, "It is God that justifieth. Who is he that condemneth?" (Rom. 8:33–34). God himself has appointed this way. So there is our first answer. God made it, and he commands us to walk along it.

So how do I answer my conscience? As my conscience confronts me with my sins, how do I answer the condemnation of God's holy law? And the answer is still adequate: "Christ is the end of the law for righteousness to every one that believeth" (Rom. 10:4). The law has been honored. He fulfilled it positively. He has borne our sins. He has borne the punishment. The law has been carried out. The punishment has been meted out. The law is satisfied. And as the law is satisfied, my conscience is satisfied. "If our heart condemn us, God is greater than our heart, and knoweth all things" (1 John 3:20). Even though we have sinned, we go to God and we believe with John that "If we confess our sins, he is faithful and just to forgive us our sins, and to cleanse us from all unrighteousness" (1 John 1:9). If he has already punished my sin in Jesus Christ, he cannot punish me again. "The blood of Jesus Christ his Son cleanseth us from all sin" (1 John 1:7).

"Well," you may say, "I believe my sins are forgiven. But my difficulty is pollution, my sense of unworthiness. When I meet great saints in a human sense, I always feel I'm unclean and unworthy, though they never say a word against me. Multiply that by infinity, and how can I stand in the presence of God?"

A great hymn writer, Thomas Binney, has faced this problem for us:

Eternal Light! Eternal Light!
How pure the soul must be
When, placed within thy searching sight,
It shrinks not, but with calm delight
Can live, and look on thee!

My friends, that is the teaching of the author of Hebrews concerning prayer. You cannot rely on yourself and your good works and your good desires or the fact that you are better than somebody else. You cannot rely upon an earthly human priesthood, a ceremonial system and a ritual that belongs to the Old Testament rather than to the New. There is only one way—"Jesus Christ, and him crucified" (1 Cor. 2:2), risen, ascended, seated at the right hand of the Glory, ever living to make intercession for us.

Beloved Christian people, we live in an age of confusion and uncertainty, an age of religious persecution, which may come to our own land as well as to every other land. We may know the trials and the tribulations and the problems of the early church and the early Christians of the first century. Indeed, even with life as it is, what is more important than knowing the way into the presence of God? We all need mercy. We all require "grace to help in time of need" (Heb. 4:16). There is only one way to get it, and that is to travel on this new and living way planned by God, made and brought into being by God the Son, mediated to us with the enabling to walk along it by the blessed Holy Spirit.

May God grant that we will all be so certain of this new and living way that we may walk upon it with such boldness and surety that we will never want to go back to something dead and passing but will ever look unto Jesus, "the author and finisher of our faith" (Heb. 12:2).

O Lord our God, we thank you for this new and living way, which your Son has consecrated for us through the veil, that is to say, his flesh. We thank you for the blood of Jesus. O God, we ask you to strengthen and deepen our faith and our knowledge of these things. Lord, teach us to see the glory and the perfection and the wonder of it all, that we may ever rejoice in it and so live for the praise of the glory of your grace. Hear us, in the name of your dear Son, our blessed Lord and Savior, Jesus Christ. Amen.

NOTES

1. The nine sermons in this book were preached in Pensacola, Florida, during Martyn Lloyd-Jones's final visit to the USA in 1969.
2. The Second World War.
3. It had been reported that a hurricane was approaching Pensacola, where these sermons were being preached. *See also*, Foreword.
4. In his poem "To a Friend," Matthew Arnold wrote of his friend, "Who saw life steadily, and saw it whole."
5. The opening words of a poem by William Wordsworth.
6. The Second World War.
7. Charles Haddon Spurgeon, "Consolation in Christ," preached December 2, 1860 at Exeter Hall, Strand.
8. Charles Haddon Spurgeon, "Predestination and Calling," preached March 6, 1859 at the Music Hall, Royal Surrey Gardens.

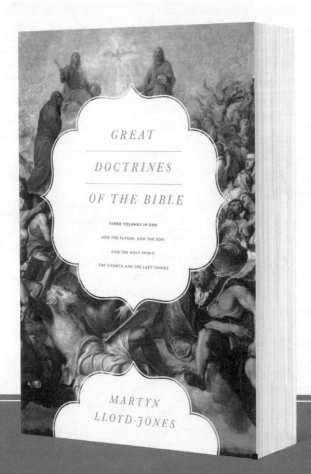

A *comprehensive* and *accessible*
systematic theology of the *Christian faith*
from *Martyn Lloyd-Jones*

This volume includes the
following three books in one:

GOD THE FATHER, GOD THE SON
GOD THE HOLY SPIRIT
THE CHURCH AND THE LAST THINGS

:: CROSSWAY

More Than Fifty Never-Before-Published Sermons by Martyn Lloyd-Jones

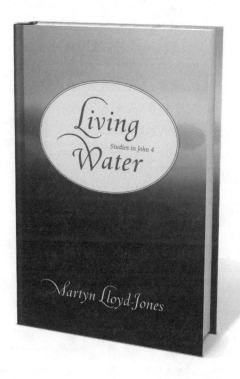

Now, for the first time, fifty-six sermons by Martyn Lloyd-Jones on John 4 are available in *Living Water*. Lloyd-Jones, known for his ability to clearly communicate profound theological concepts, digs into this familiar passage from John's Gospel, exposing fresh layers of truth.

Jesus answered and said unto her, Whosoever drinketh of this water shall thirst again: but whosoever drinketh of the water that I shall give him shall never thirst; but the water that I shall give him shall be in him a well of water springing up into everlasting life.

John 4:13–14 KJV

:: CROSSWAY

"WHY AM I THE WAY I AM?"

"WHY IS LIFE SO HARD?"

"IS THERE ANY HOPE?"

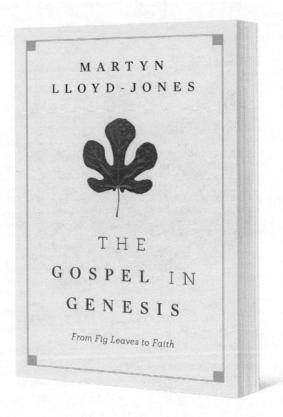

In this series of never-before-published sermons, Martyn Lloyd-Jones preaches the gospel of Jesus Christ from the early chapters of Genesis. These nine sermons feature the eternal perspective, sense of urgency, and unapologetic honesty that characterized his preaching.

In *The Gospel in Genesis*, Lloyd-Jones seeks to awaken nonbelievers to their lostness and embolden Christians to believe firmly the only gospel that offers answers to life's biggest questions.

:: CROSSWAY